NEW ESSAYS ON
THE HOUSE OF MIRTH

Edith Wharton's *The House of Mirth* captured the attention of a large portion of the American reading public when it was published in a serial version in *Scribner's* in 1905 and then as a hardback in October of that year. Wharton's story of Lily Bart, a "social parasite," according to Edmund Wilson, "on the fringes of the very rich," topped one best-seller list for four months. The novel sealed the author's reputation as one of the major English-language fiction writers of her generation. Each of the four essays collected in this volume of The American Novel series makes distinctive new claims for the historical, critical, and theoretical significance of Wharton's seminal work.

Deborah Esch, Associate Professor of English at the University of Toronto, is the author of *In the Event: Reading Journalism, Reading Theory* (1999) and *The Brevity of Life* (forthcoming). She is coeditor of *Critical Encounters* (1994) and the Norton Critical Edition of Henry James's *The Turn of the Screw* (1999) and has published a range of articles on nineteenth- and twentieth-century American and comparative literature, literary theory, media culture, and visual art.

*   The American Novel   *

GENERAL EDITOR

Emory Elliott
University of California, Riverside

Other books in the series:

New Essays on
The House of Mirth

Edited by

Deborah Esch

CAMBRIDGE
UNIVERSITY PRESS

PUBLISHED BY THE PRESS SYNDICATE OF THE UNIVERSITY OF CAMBRIDGE
The Pitt Building, Trumpington Street, Cambridge, United Kingdom

CAMBRIDGE UNIVERSITY PRESS
The Edinburgh Building, Cambridge CB2 2RU, UK
40 West 20th Street, New York, NY 10011-4211, USA
10 Stamford Road, Oakleigh, VIC 3166, Australia
Ruiz de Alarcón 13, 28014 Madrid, Spain
Dock House, The Waterfront, Cape Town 8001, South Africa

http://www.cambridge.org

© Cambridge University Press 2001

First published 2001

Printed in the United States of America

Typeface Meridien 10/13 pt.   *System* QuarkXPress [BTS]

A catalog record for this book is available from the British Library.

Library of Congress Cataloging in Publication data

New essays on The house of mirth / edited by Deborah Esch.
p. cm. – (The American novel)
Includes bibliographical references.
(ISBN 0-521-37231-3 – ISBN 0-521-37833-8 (pbk.)
1. Wharton, Edith, 1862–1937. House of mirth. 2. Social classes in literature.
3. Single women in literature. I. Esch, Deborah, 1954– . II. Series.
PS3545.H16 H6836 2001
813'.52 – dc21   00-025948

ISBN   0 521 37231 3   hardback
ISBN   0 521 37833 8   paperback

Contents

Contents

Series Editor's Preface

In literary criticism the last twenty-five years have been particularly fruitful. Since the rise of the New Criticism in the 1950s, which focused attention of critics and readers upon the text itself – apart from history, biography, and society – there has emerged a wide variety of critical methods which have brought to literary works a rich diversity of perspectives: social, historical, political, psychological, economic, ideological, and philosophical. While attention to the text itself, as taught by the New Critics, remains at the core of contemporary interpretation, the widely shared assumption that works of art generate many different kinds of interpretations has opened up possibilities for new readings and new meanings.

Before this critical revolution, many works of American literature had come to be taken for granted by earlier generations of readers as having an established set of recognized interpretations. There was a sense among many students that the canon was established and that the larger thematic and interpretative issues had been decided. The task of the new reader was to examine the ways in which elements such as structure, style, and imagery contributed to each novel's acknowledged purpose. But recent criticism has brought these old assumptions into question and has thereby generated a wide variety of original, and often quite surprising, interpretations of the classics, as well as of rediscovered works such as Kate Chopin's *The Awakening*, which has only recently entered the canon of works that scholars and critics study and that teachers assign their students.

The aim of The American Novel series is to provide students of American literature and culture with introductory critical guides to American novels and other important texts now widely read and studied. Usually devoted to a single work, each volume begins with an introduction by the volume editor, a distinguished authority on the text. The introduction presents details of the work's composition, publication history, and contemporary reception, as well as a survey of the major critical trends and readings from first publication to the present. This overview is followed by four or five original essays, specifically commissioned from senior scholars of established reputation and from out-standing younger critics. Each essay presents a distinct point of view, and together they constitute a forum of interpretative methods and of the best contemporary ideas on each text.

It is our hope that these volumes will convey the vitality of current critical work in American literature, generate new insights and excitement for students of American literature, and inspire new respect for and new perspectives upon these major literary texts.

Emory Elliott
University of California, Riverside

1

Introduction

DEBORAH ESCH

1

Inscribed in a recollection by Philomène de la Forest-Divonne of an afternoon visit to the Pavillon Colombe in St. Brice in 1935 or 1936 is another reminiscence: that of her host and longtime friend, Edith Wharton: " 'I was writing little stories when I was four,' she said to me, not at all boasting about her gift, but also not seeking to deny it."[1] Months before her death, the accomplished author made her visitor "a participant in her earliest memories," and recalled fabricating fictions even before she learned, at the age of six, to read. The nascent career took a decisive turn during Edith Newbold Jones's twelfth year, when, according to her biographer R. W. B. Lewis, she "decided to write a story: she would, that is, set down one of her inventions on paper. She would 'make up'" (Lewis, 29–30). Taking her own immediate circumstances as point of departure, she again put pen to paper: " 'Oh, how do you do, Mrs. Brown?' said Mrs. Tomkins. 'If only I had known you were going to call, I should have tidied up the drawing room'" (quoted in Lewis, 30).

The reception of this early attempt was swift and severe: Lucretia Jones promptly returned the page her daughter had shyly proffered with the curt judgment that "drawing rooms are always tidy" (Lewis, 30). In the wake of her mother's response, the young Edith turned her talents to poetry, thereby earning the approval of her parents and eventually publishing a handful of poems. After a three-year hiatus, she reverted to narrative fiction with a secret but sustained effort, a novella of thirty thousand words entitled *Fast and Loose*. As Shari Benstock observes, "An irony of Edith's early literary development is that she *wrote* a

1

novella before she had ever *read* one."[2] This time around, she assumed as her own the function of unforgiving critic and "began at once to deprecate the work. She wrote a number of mock reviews, attributed to various New York and London periodicals, each denouncing [the novella] in uncompromising terms. . . . [A]dopting the authoritative voice of *The Nation*, she declared that 'It is false charity to reader and writer to mince matters. The English of it is that every character is a failure, the plot a vacuum, the style spiritless, the dialogue vague, the sentiment weak and the whole thing a fiasco!'" (quoted in Lewis, 31). With this harsh anatomy, Edith Newbold Jones cast herself in the dual role of storyteller and critical reader at the tender age of fifteen.

The biographer's reconstruction of these early episodes is remarkably consistent with Wharton's own account, in her memoir *A Backward Glance* (1934), of the composition of *The House of Mirth*. "Fate had planted me in New York," she relates, "and my instinct as a story-teller counselled me to use the material nearest to hand, and most familiarly my own."[3] After the fact, the critic elaborates the storyteller's dilemma:

There could be no greater critical ineptitude than to judge a novel according to *what it ought to have been about*. . . . As a matter of fact, there are but two essential rules: one, that the novelist should deal only with what is within his reach, literally or figuratively (in most cases the two are synonymous), and the other that the value of a subject depends almost wholly on what the author sees in it, and how deeply he is able to see *into* it. Almost – but not quite; for there are certain subjects too shallow to yield anything to the most searching gaze. I had always felt this, and now my problem was how to make use of a subject – fashionable New York – which, of all others, seemed most completely to fall within the condemned category. There it was before me, in all its flatness and futility, asking to be dealt with as the theme most available to my hand, since I had been steeped in it from infancy, and should not have to get it up out of note-books and encyclopedias – and yet! (*A Backward Glance*, 206–7)

The autobiographical account goes on to formulate the predicament posed by the most familiar material and its attendant thematics: "how to extract from such a subject the typical human significance which is the story-teller's reason for telling one story rather than another" (*A Backward Glance*, 207). More particularly,

In what aspect could a society of irresponsible pleasure-seekers be said to have, on the "old woe of the world," any deeper bearing than the people composing such a society could guess? The answer was that a frivolous society can acquire dramatic significance only through what its frivolity destroys. Its tragic implication lies in its power of debasing people and ideals. The answer, in short, was my heroine, Lily Bart. (*A Backward Glance*, 207)

With the critical question of "typical human significance" – which is to say, of a story's meaning and its figuration – provisionally articulated and answered, the narrative acquired the requisite momentum. The novel had been promised in advance to *Scribner's Magazine*, and the deadline moved forward to January 1905 when the novel that was to have preceded it was not submitted in time. *A Backward Glance* belatedly registers the alarm of a fledgling novelist torn between "critical dissatisfaction with the work, and the distractions of a busy and hospitable life, full of friends and travel, reading and gardening" (*A Backward Glance*, 207), to say nothing of the repeated nervous collapses of her husband: "The first chapters of my tale would have to appear almost at once, and it must be completed within four or five months! I have always been a slow worker, and was then a very inexperienced one, and I was to be put to the severest test to which a novelist can be subjected: my novel was to be exposed to public comment before I had worked it out to its climax" (*A Backward Glance*, 208). Just what that climax would be was not in doubt: "My last page is always latent in my first; but the intervening windings of the way always become clear only as I write, and now I was asked to gallop over them before I had even traced them out! I had expected to devote another year or eighteen months to the task, instead of which I was asked to be ready within six months; and nothing short of 'the hand of God' must be suffered to interrupt my labors, since my first chapters would already be in print!" (*A Backward Glance*, 208).

Under the enforced "discipline of the daily task" (*A Backward Glance*, 208), Wharton managed to deliver the manuscript to the publisher on schedule. She recollects her gratitude in the aftermath of her trial by fire: "It was good to be turned from a drifting amateur into a professional; but that was nothing compared to the effect on my imagination of systematic daily effort.... When the book was done I remember saying to myself: 'I don't yet know how to write a novel; *but I know how to find out how to*'" (*A Backward Glance*, 209).

2

In its serial version, *The House of Mirth* appeared in eleven installments in *Scribner's*, running from January to November 1905, and finding a receptive public; "readers who arrived late at their local newsstand found no available copy."[4] Wharton collected $5,000 for the serial rights. The book was initially published in New York on October 14, 1905, in an edition of 40,000 copies. Readers paid $1.50 for the volume, and Wharton's contract stipulated royalties of fifteen percent. As Lewis notes, "by the end of 1905 she had been paid $7,000 against accrued royalties of more than $30,000" (Lewis, 151). The tax-free figure translates to well over $500,000 today.

The House of Mirth, in other words, was from the first a formidable commodity. Ten days after the novel appeared, the publisher notified Wharton that "so far we have not sold many over 30,000, but perhaps that will satisfy your expectations for the first fortnight" (quoted in Lewis, 151). The author recorded in her diary a subsequent printing of 20,000 by October 30, and an additional 20,000 on November 11. As the year drew to a close, 140,000 copies were in print, and Charles Scribner could report that *The House of Mirth* was enjoying "the most rapid sale of any book ever published by Scribner" (quoted in Lewis, 151; Benstock, "A Critical History," 310).

Contemporary reviews of the best-selling novel (it held the top spot on one list for four months) were on the whole more concerned with evaluation than analysis, and with the answer to Wharton's critical question ("in short . . . my heroine, Lily Bart") than with the possibilities inscribed in the question itself. For the most part, the work won praise from American as well as English reviewers (it appeared under the Macmillan imprint in Britain), whether they read it as realist chronicle or mannerist satire. Unfavorable responses focused on the hopelessness of the tale of Lily Bart's inexorable descent from privilege to destitution, and debated whether her death was the necessary price of the author's moral claim. Others took Wharton to task for her unsparing portrayal of New York society: either for not presenting finer exemplars of humanity in her chosen context, or simply for having selected in the first place material "utterly unsuitable for conversion into literature," which "demands all that such society has not – ideas, intellectual interests, sentiment, passion, humor, wit, tact, and grace."[5] (This assessment in *The Nation* thus anticipates aspects of Wharton's own subsequent judgment about her subject matter in *A Backward Glance*.) But a survey of early critical responses to the novel makes clear that even the most hostile contributors to the controversy surrounding the publication of *The House of Mirth* sought somewhat vainly to find fault with what was widely regarded as a work of great merit.[6] "Amid the favorable, the issue was whether *The House of Mirth* could be adjudged a masterpiece or whether it fell just short of that final accolade" (Lewis, 154). *The Saturday Review* summarily pronounced the work "one of the few novels which can claim to rank as literature" (Ammons, 313).

If *The House of Mirth* sealed its author's reputation as one of the major English-language novelists of her generation, and as a worthy "historian of the American society of her time," Wharton's restlessness as a storyteller and social critic would thenceforth transport her far from the New York of her day.[7] In only one other novel, *The Custom of the Country* (1913), would she return to that familiar time and place. At her death in 1937, she had been living as an expatriate in France for several decades, and was arguably best known to a new generation of readers as the author of *Ethan Frome* (1911), which had become available in an inexpensive and widely circulated library edition.

3

The warm reception that had greeted most of Wharton's fiction in America as well as Europe cooled significantly in the 1930s, when, as Benstock observes, "her social chronicles, *The House of Mirth* first among them, were judged as mere 'curiosities' – nostalgic reminiscences . . . of a bygone age rather than condemnations of modern mores. With the rise of fascism and the fear of war in Europe . . . Wharton's comedies had little to say to a generation that anticipated the collapse of civilization" ("A Critical History," 315). But in "Justice to Edith Wharton," an essay written shortly after the author's death, Edmund Wilson sought to revive Wharton's flagging critical fortunes, and specifically "to throw into relief the achievements which did make her important during a period – say, 1905–1917 – when there were few American writers worth reading" (Wilson, 19). In the context of its measured defense of the novelist ("she was one of the few Americans of her day who cared enough about serious literature to take the risks of trying to make some contribution to it" [Wilson, 30]), the essay does at best equivocal justice to *The House of Mirth*: Wilson writes that "[t]he language and some of the machinery . . . seem old-fashioned and rather melodramatic today; but the book has some originality and power, with its chronicle of a social parasite on the fringes of the very rich . . . and finding a window open only twice, at the beginning and at the end of the book, on a world where all the values are not money values" (Wilson, 21).

It would fall to a subsequent critic to make a more compelling case for the persistent interest and lasting value of *The House of Mirth*, and arguably "to show Mrs. Wharton in her proper place in the main stream of American literature."[8] Diana Trilling's "*The House of Mirth* Revisited," which appeared in 1962, acknowledges that the quarter-century following Wharton's death "has delivered the mortal blow to the society in which she came of literary age, so that it is no small wonder that her extraordinary work has passed into the archeological shadows and that now, where she is known at all outside university English courses, it is merely, and pejoratively, as a society lady become society author" (Trilling, 103). But Trilling's polemic overturns this conventional wisdom, arguing that Wharton "knew the reality of class as no theoretical Marxist or social egalitarian can know it: not speculatively but in her bones" (Trilling, 105). Read in this light, *The House of Mirth* is for Trilling "nothing if not a novel about social stratification and the consequences of breaking the taboos of class," and indeed ranks as "one of the most telling indictments of a social system based on the chance distribution of wealth, and therefore of social privilege, that has ever been put on paper" (Trilling, 105, 106).

In crucial respects, Trilling's revaluation of the novel paved the way for later readers who would bring a range of theoretical approaches to bear on Wharton's text. In the aftermath of the New Criticism and the formalist tendencies that predominated in North American literary studies in the 1940s and 1950s (and that had little investment in, and as little to say about, the ethical, social, and historical stakes of a work like *The House of Mirth*), critics of the novel returned to the "issues that had drawn the attention of its earliest readers: the tension between character and situation, and the influence of gender, social class, race and the marketplace in shaping the moral climate of society – and, by extension, the literature it produced" (Benstock, "A Critical History," 317). Something of a "renaissance" (Benstock's term) or "revolution" (Annette Zilvermatt's) in Wharton studies took place following the opening in 1967 of the Yale archive, and the appointment by the Wharton estate of R. W. B. Lewis as official biographer (his *Edith Wharton* apppeared in 1975, and garnered the Pulitzer Prize, the National Book Critics Circle Award, and Columbia University's Bancroft Prize for history). In the subsequent quarter-century, scholars and critics, many of them representing a diversity of feminisms informed by psychoanalysis, historical materialism, and deconstruction, have re-revisited *The House of Mirth*, generating a substantial and varied body of criticism on the novel.

Since the late 1970s, several landmark studies have sought to establish the interpretive authority of approaches that would do greater justice to Wharton's life and work. *A Feast of Words*, Cynthia Griffin Wolff's psychobiography, appeared in 1977, forging a path for further psychoanalytically oriented accounts by Lev Raphael, Barbara White, David Holbrook, and Gloria Ehrlich. In 1980, Elizabeth Ammons's *Edith Wharton's Argument with America* attempted to situate Wharton's oeuvre in the context of a feminist resistance to patriarchy and its institutions, notably marriage. Shari Benstock included Wharton in *Women of the Left Bank*, an historical account of expatriate modernism in France published in 1986.

Increasing scholarly interest in Wharton found fresh resources and outlets with the founding of the Edith Wharton Society and its journal, the *Edith Wharton Review*. In 1988, Scribner's published *The Letters of Edith Wharton*, a volume of her correspondence from 1902 to 1937 edited by R. W. B. Lewis and Nancy Lewis. A year later, the Beinecke Library recatalogued its Edith Wharton Collection, affording readier access to the significant archival holdings at Yale. Alongside the renewal of academic investment, popular interest in the author's life and work has likewise flourished. Evidence for this wider appeal includes the several films based on her fiction (including *The Age of Innocence*, directed by Martin Scorsese) and a host of articles in architecture, landscape, design, and travel periodicals as well as in mainstream literary reviews. Affordable paperback editions of *The House of Mirth*, including Ammons's Norton Critical Edition (1990) and Benstock's volume for the series Case Studies in Contemporary Criticism (1994), have made available to teachers and students not only authoritative texts of the novel, but valuable critical histories and contextual material as well as recent interpretive accounts.

4

It is fair to say that critical responses to *The House of Mirth*, from contemporary reviews to the most recent theoretically oriented interpretations, stand in some relation to the question posed by Wharton in her account of writing the novel in *A Backward Glance*: "how to extract from such a subject the typical human significance which is the story-teller's reason for telling one story rather than another." For the dilemma (again, in the last analysis one of narrative meaning and its figuration) is double: if it begins as the writer's problem, it inevitably becomes the reader's as well. And as such, it is thematized in the story of Lily Bart, the novel's central figure, who "was so evidently the victim of the civilization which had produced her, that the links of her bracelet seemed like manacles chaining her to her fate."[9]

At pivotal junctures in the unfolding of that fate, Wharton's heroine finds herself doubled, or more precisely self-divided. When a tacit comparison between Lawrence Selden and Percy Gryce prompts Lily to choose Selden and a certain freedom in the present over Gryce and a predictable future ("It was that comparison which was her undoing" [I, 5, 44]), we read that

There were in her at that moment two beings, one drawing deep breaths of freedom and exhilaration, the other gasping for air in a little black prison-house of fears. But gradually the captive's gasps grew fainter, or the other paid less heed to them; the horizon expanded, the air grew stronger, and the free spirit quivered for flight. (I, 6, 52)

The self-division proves permanent (as Selden tells Lily much later, "The difference is in yourself – it will always be there" [II, 12, 239]). And over the course of its narration, Wharton's language spells out the constitutive temporal dimension that renders its structure allegorical. That structure is readable, for example, in Lily's reaction to the traumatic encounter with Gus Trenor in Book I, Chapter 13:

"I can't think – I can't think," she moaned, and leaned her head against the rattling side of the cab. She seemed a stranger to herself, or rather there were two selves in her, the one she had always known, and a new abhorrent being to which it found itself chained. She had once picked up, in a house where she was staying, a translation of the *Eumenides*, and her imagination had been seized by the high terror of the scene where Orestes, in the cave of the oracle, finds his implacable huntresses asleep, and snatches an hour's repose. Yes, the Furies might sometimes sleep, but they were there, always there in the dark corners, and now they were awake and the iron clang of their wings was in her brain. . . . She opened her eyes and saw the streets passing – the familiar alien streets. All she looked on was the same and yet changed. There was a great gulf fixed between today and yesterday. Everything in the past seemed simple and natural, full of daylight – and she was alone in the

place of darkness and pollution. – Alone! It was the loneliness that frightened her. Her eyes fell on an illuminated clock at a street corner, and
she saw that the hands marked the half-hour after eleven. . . . Oh, the
slow cold drip of the minutes on her head! (I, 13, 117–18)

Something of Lily's predicament, here tellingly figured in terms
of her own past experience of reading at the remove of translation, is discernible even to her casual acquaintances. In the
opening chapter of the second book, Carrie Fisher remarks to
Selden, "Sometimes . . . I think it's just flightiness – and sometimes I think it's because, at heart, she despises the things she's
trying for. And it's the difficulty of deciding that makes her such
an interesting study" (II, 1, 148).

If several generations of critics have confronted some version of the "difficulty of deciding" about Lily Bart, it is the
fictive heroine's contemporary and friend Gerty Farish who
poses the problem in the terms most characteristic of Wharton
herself: those of telling, and attending to, stories. Following
the revelation that Lily has been betrayed by Bertha Dorset
and disinherited by her aunt, Gerty anxiously forces the
question:

"But what *is* your story, Lily? I don't believe any one knows it yet."
"My story? – I don't believe I know it myself. You see I never thought
of preparing a version in advance . . . and if I had, I don't think I should
take the trouble to use it now." . . .
"I don't want a version prepared in advance – but I want you to tell
me exactly what happened from the beginning."
"From the beginning?" . . . "Dear Gerty, how little imagination you
good people have! Why, the beginning was in my cradle, I suppose – in
the way I was brought up, and the things I was taught to care for. Or
no – I won't blame anybody for my faults. I'll say it was in my blood,
that I got it from some wicked pleasure-loving ancestress. . . . You asked
me just now for the truth – well, the truth about any girl is that once
she's talked about she's done for . . ." (II, 4, 176)

Shortly thereafter, Simon Rosedale formally withdraws his
marriage proposal in terms that ironically echo Lily's, and under-
score their stakes: the relation between "the truth" (i.e., what
happened) and the stories to which the truth's occlusion gives
rise:

"I don't believe the stories about you – I don't *want* to believe them. But they're there, and my not believing them ain't going to alter the situation.". . .

"If they are not true . . . doesn't *that* alter the situation?". . .

"I believe it does in novels; but I'm certain it don't in real life. You know that as well as I do: if we're speaking the truth, let's speak the whole truth." (II, 7, 199–200)

Again ironically, it is only at the end of Lily's life and its narrative that Selden finally grasps the same stakes:

It was true, then, that she had taken money from Trenor; but true also . . . that the obligation had been intolerable to her, and that at the first opportunity she had freed herself from it. . . .

That was all he knew – all he could hope to unravel of the story. The mute lips on the pillow refused him more than this – unless indeed they had told him the rest in the kiss they had left upon his forehead. Yes, he could now read into that farewell all that his heart craved to find there. (II, 14, 255)

Gerty's futile plea to be told "exactly what happened from the beginning" locates the point where story would coincide with history, understood as the material specificity of the event. In effect, her words stamp Lily's story – *The House of Mirth* itself – as an allegory of history, a narrative that alludes to the anteriority of events that it cannot fully recuperate or comprehend. (This is arguably figured in the effects of the chloral on which Lily comes to depend: "But in the sleep which the phial procured she sank far below such half-waking visitations, sank into the depths of dreamless annihilation from which she woke each morning with an obliterated past" [II, 10, 230].) Once again, the narrative thematizes at several junctures the elusiveness of the event: of what happened, or happens, or will happen. Prior to Bertha Dorset's fateful banishment of Lily in Monte Carlo, Selden offers a half-hearted warning:

"I stopped over to see you – to beg of you to leave the yacht."

The eyes she turned on him showed a quick gleam of her former fear. "To leave – ? What do you mean? What has happened?"

The glare from the jeweller's window, deepening the pallour of her face, gave to its delicate lines the sharpness of a tragic mask. "Nothing will, I am sure." . . .

11

"You have yourself to think of, you know –" to which, with a strangeness in her voice, she answered, meeting his eyes: "If you knew how
little difference that makes!"

"Oh, well, nothing *will* happen," he said, more for his own reassurance than for hers; and "Nothing, nothing, of course!" she valiantly
assented, as they turned to overtake their companions. (II, 3, 167)

A comparable note of "foreboding" attends the final exchange
between Lily and Selden, immediately preceding her death by
overdose, when the possibility of a love that might alter both
their fates is relegated by the heroine herself to an irrevocable
past.

She looked at him gently. "Do you remember what you said to me once?
That you could help me only by loving me? Well – you did love me for
a moment; and it helped me. It has always helped me. But the moment
is gone – it was I who let it go. And one must go on living. Goodbye."

She laid her hand on his, and they looked at each other with a kind
of solemnity, as though they stood in the presence of death. Something
in truth lay dead between them – the love she had killed in him and
could no longer call to life. But something lived between them also, and
leaped up in her like an imperishable flame: it was the love his love had
kindled, the passion of her soul for his.

In its light everything else dwindled and fell away from her. She
understood now that she could not go forth and leave her old self with
him: that self must indeed live on in his presence, but it must still continue to be hers. . . .

"Lily," he said in a low voice, "you musn't speak in this way. I can't
let you go without knowing what you mean to do. Things may change
– but they don't pass. You can never go out of my life."

She met his eyes with an illumined look. "No," she said, "I see
that now. Let us always be friends. Then I shall feel safe, whatever
happens." . . .

"Whatever happens? What do you mean? What is going to happen?"
She turned away quietly and walked toward the hearth.
"Nothing at present." (II, 12, 241)

What is necessarily lacking in the language of *The House of
Mirth* – the event itself – is what continues to yield a multiplicity of stories, both within the novel and about it. Coming to
terms with Wharton's narrative thus remains a task irreducible
to telling or reading a story in the singular, one "rather than"

another. The four essays collected in the present volume, each of which makes new claims for the novel's critical and theoretical significance, attest to this irreducibility. To borrow Wharton's own phrasing in *A Backward Glance*, if with the advantage of their cumulative insight we still retain some sense that we "don't yet know how to" read *The House of Mirth*, we undoubtedly know better *"how to find out how to."*

NOTES

1. R. W. B. Lewis, *Edith Wharton: A Biography* (New York: Harper and Row, 1975), 527.
2. Shari Benstock, "Introduction: Biographical and Historical Contexts," in Edith Wharton, *The House of Mirth*, ed. Shari Benstock (Boston: Bedford Books, 1994), 5.
3. Edith Wharton, *A Backward Glance* (London: Century, 1987), 206.
4. Shari Benstock, "A Critical History of *The House of Mirth*," in Wharton, *The House of Mirth*, ed. Benstock, 310.
5. *The Nation* (London) 81 (1905): 447–48; quoted in Edith Wharton, *The House of Mirth*, ed. Elizabeth Ammons (New York: Norton, 1990), 312.
6. See the excerpts from a number of contemporary reviews reproduced in Ammons's Norton Critical Edition of the novel, 307–13, and the admirable summary of early responses in Benstock, "A Critical History," 310–14.
7. Edmund Wilson, "Justice to Edith Wharton," in *Edith Wharton*, ed. Irving Howe (Englewood Cliffs, N.J.: Prentice-Hall, 1962), 19.
8. Diana Trilling, *"The House of Mirth* Revisited," in *Edith Wharton*, ed. Howe, 103.
9. This and all further references to the novel throughout this volume are to Ammons's Norton Critical Edition (Book I, Chapter 1, page 8).

2

The Conspicuous Wasting of Lily Bart

RUTH BERNARD YEAZELL

Few fictional heroines have been as consistently under observation as Lily Bart, and few heroes have proved such consistent observers as Lawrence Selden.[1] Yet he scarcely registers her most notable performance. Indeed, by the time that Lily drops Bertha Dorset's letters into Selden's fireplace, the very inconspicuousness of the act testifies to its moral significance. In "a world where conspicuousness passed for distinction, and the society column had become the roll of fame" (II, 3, 168), Lily unobtrusively destroys the evidence that would threaten her principal enemy with exposure – a parcel of adulterous love letters from Bertha to Selden that first came into her hands suitably wrapped in "dirty newspaper" (I, 9, 80). Though Bertha herself has dramatically staged Lily's expulsion from fashionable society in a "strident setting" illuminated by "a special glare of publicity" and duly recorded by "the watchful pen" of the gossip columnist (II, 3, 168, 169), Lily burns the letters in a tranquil room softly lit against the "gathering darkness" (II, 12, 237), and with only the uncomprehending Selden for witness: "When she rose he fancied that he saw her draw something from her dress and drop it into the fire; but he hardly noticed the gesture at the time" (II, 12, 241). As it happens, this will also prove the last time that he sees her alive.[2]

The House of Mirth opens on a very different vision of its heroine, as Selden's attention is suddenly arrested by the sight of Lily amid the afternoon rush of Grand Central Station. Though the two are already well acquainted, the setting of their first meeting emphasizes Lily's power to draw attention merely as an anonymous spectacle, a spectacle all the more attractive by virtue of its difference from the hurrying and crowded scene. "Miss Bart was a figure to arrest even the suburban traveller rushing to his last train," the narrator remarks. "Her vivid head, relieved against the dull tints of the crowd, made her more conspicuous than in a ball-room" (I, 1, 5). By the close of the chapter, however, Lily's impulsive acceptance of Selden's invitation to tea in his bachelor quarters will twice subject her to scrutiny of a more unwelcome kind. "There were a thousand chances to one against her meeting anybody," she thinks sensibly enough on leaving Selden's apartment, but a woman who is conspicuous in Grand Central Station will inevitably attract observation wherever she goes; and in a pattern that will be repeated at several crucial moments in the novel, her slightest deviation from propriety seems guaranteed to turn the anonymous streets of the modern city into the oppressively close byways of an inquisitive small town. Though at first there is "no one in sight . . . but a char-woman" who looks up "curiously" as she passes (I, 1, 13), the woman's stare follows Lily so persistently that she flushes under the look – and as if help in old New York had already become uncannily scarce, the same woman will later reappear scrubbing the staircase of the house where Lily lives with her aunt. And no sooner does Lily reach the sidewalk, of course, than she encounters the gaze of Simon Rosedale, the ambitious Jew whose "small sidelong eyes . . . gave him the air of appraising people as if they were bric-a-brac." Caught off guard by "the sudden intimacy of his smile," she tries to cover herself by claiming to have been visiting her dressmaker (I, 1, 15), only to have the obviousness of her social lie ironically underlined by Rosedale's revelation that he just happens to own Selden's building. As we shall see, Lily's attempted cover-up involves a further irony, though one that the novelist does not make explicit, since dressmakers, in this world of "rich and conspicuous people" (I, 5, 42–3), at best produce a showy variety of concealment.

Published only a half-dozen years after Thorstein Veblen's mordant analysis of the phenomenon he termed "conspicuous consumption," Wharton's second novel rivals *The Theory of the Leisure Class* (1899) both as sociology and as satire.[3] For Wharton, as for Veblen, the study of the leisure class is above all a study of waste. In a frequently quoted passage from her autobiography, the novelist even suggests that Lily Bart herself exists primarily as a measure of what her culture throws away: because "a frivolous society can acquire dramatic significance only through what its frivolity destroys," *The House of Mirth* apparently acquired its heroine.[4] Like Veblen, Wharton represents a world in which people acquire and maintain status by openly displaying how much they can afford to waste; and like Veblen, she knows that the crowded conditions of modern urban life compel them to make such displays all the more conspicuously. In order to impress the "transient observers" who rush past one in the modern city, Veblen argues, "and to retain one's self-complacency under their observation, the signature of one's pecuniary strength should be written in characters which he who runs may read."[5] So in Wharton's novel, the annual New York Horse Show occasions "a human display of the same costly and highstepping kind as circled daily about its ring"; and Mrs. Gormer, one of the newest of the status-seeking nouveaux riches, seizes the opportunity to advertise her wealth by choosing "the most conspicuous box the house afforded" (II, 8, 203). And while *The House of Mirth* begins when the attention of the rushing crowd is caught by a woman's "conspicuous" beauty rather than by a sign of "pecuniary strength," both Wharton and Veblen make clear how the one can stand in for the other – how the woman of the leisure class serves to represent the financial strength of her "master," as Veblen puts it, by being herself "the chief ornament" in his collection and by vicariously "perform[ing]" conspicuous leisure and consumption for him. Though Veblen rarely approaches this arrangement without his characteristic irony – "the male head of the household," as he dryly remarks, "is not currently spoken of as its ornament"[6] – it is perhaps not surprising that the novelist proves more alert to the double binds that constrain woman's performance, or that she registers more fully than the economist the psychic costs such performance exacts.

As Veblen describes them, people are insatiably emulative animals, always defining their own success by "invidious" comparisons to others. If the desire to one-up the next person is not the only reason people seek wealth in *The Theory of the Leisure*

Class, it dominates all the rest: in Veblen's speculative account of human history, the competition for wealth has simply come to replace more obvious kinds of "predatory activity" as the arena in which men struggle to prove themselves one another's superiors. Even in a preindustrial age, Veblen contends, the display of property had a symbolic function, but where men used to demonstrate their greater strength in battle or the hunt by showing off the trophies they had managed to capture, they now display their accumulated property as "a trophy of successes scored in the game of ownership." Though Veblen admits that people can also be motivated merely by the comfort and security wealth brings, he immediately reminds us that even "the standard of sufficiency in these respects is in turn greatly affected by the habit of pecuniary emulation." One knows what one "needs," in other words, only by copying others – and one always wants more than one needs in order to surpass them. The theorist of the leisure class undoubtedly lacks the novelist's power of vivid representation, but peering from behind his dry and abstract vocabulary are people also constantly watching one another. "In order to gain and to hold the esteem of men," he typically writes, "it is not sufficient merely to possess wealth or power. The wealth or power must be put in evidence" (Veblen, 28, 32, 36).

In order to gain and hold such esteem most effectively, however, a man should also give as little indication as possible of having labored for the wealth that he puts in evidence. In "archaic" culture, as Veblen hypothesizes it, male hunters and warriors rigorously distinguished their activity from the menial tasks they assigned to women; and a similar "repugnance for the vulgar forms of labour" continued to make itself felt when people passed from the predatory to the industrial stage. Even in the days when the hunt contributed significantly to the sustenance of the group, he argues, men regarded it as a ceremonial and honorific activity more than a productive one; but as soon as settled agriculture made people no longer dependent on various forms of predatory exploit for their livelihood, the distinction became even sharper. Indeed, "from this point on, the characteristic feature of leisure-class life is a conspicuous exemption from all useful employment." Though a nineteenth-century gentleman might well engage in the ritual entertainment of the hunt – or for that matter go to war – he kept his status as gentleman precisely by showing that he was not involved in productive labor. Note that Veblen takes care to speak of "a conspicuous exemption from all *useful* employment" (emphasis added): like everyone else, even a gentleman must somehow occupy his time, but in order to prove he has no need to work, he must occupy it nonproductively. As Veblen frequently observes, leisure is itself a kind of employment, and his chapter on "Conspicuous Leisure" amusingly details some of the "quasi-scholarly or quasi-artistic accomplishments" that commonly serve as evidence that one has been engaged in just such an "unproductive expenditure of time": "the knowledge of the dead languages and the occult sciences; of correct spelling; of syntax and prosody; of the various forms of domestic music and other household art; of the latest proprieties of dress, furniture, and equipage; of games, sports, and fancy-bred animals, such as dogs and racehorses" (Veblen, 37, 40, 45).

The reader of *The House of Mirth* might well wish to add to this list a knowledge of Americana – especially as acquired by wealthy collectors like the Gryces. "It seems so odd to want to pay a lot for an ugly badly-printed book that one is never going to read!" Lily exclaims when her hopes of marrying the Gryce heir prompt her to quiz Selden about the subject; but the elegant wastefulness of the collector's knowledge is all the more evident because his books are not generally acquired, as Selden observes, in order to be read (I, 1, 11). Percy Gryce, we are told, takes as much pride in the collection "as though it had been his own work," but of course the very fact that it has not been his own work – he has inherited it from an uncle – only underlines his position as a gentleman. Timid and shy, Percy himself shrinks from public encounters, but the "personal complacency" that he feels whenever he chances on any reference to the Gryce Americana (I, 2, 19) is nonetheless exactly the sort of emotion to which Veblen alludes when he discusses how people constantly engage in "invidious comparison" in order to determine "the relative degrees of complacency with which they may legitimately be contemplated by themselves and by others":[7]

Anxious as he was to avoid personal notice, he took, in the printed mention of his name, a pleasure so exquisite and excessive that it seemed a compensation for his shrinking from publicity.

To enjoy the sensation as often as possible, he subscribed to all the reviews dealing with book-collecting in general, and American history in particular, and as allusions to his library abounded in the pages of these journals, which formed his only reading, he came to regard himself as figuring prominently in the public eye, and to enjoy the thought of the interest which would be excited if the persons he met in the street, or sat among in travelling, were suddenly to be told that he was the possessor of the Gryce Americana. (I, 2, 20)

Only his drastically limited reading could sustain Percy Gryce's illusion of prominence, but his relation to the book-collecting journals caricatures what the novel elsewhere treats with greater seriousness – the way in which "the public eye" is multiplied and magnified through the power of the printed word and of still more modern media like film. Whether or not Veblen intended to conjure up the image of newspaper headlines when he suggested that in the modern city "the signature of one's pecuniary strength should be written in characters which he who runs may read," Wharton knew that the culture of conspicuous leisure and conspicuous consumption was also increasingly a culture of mass publicity, and in *The House of Mirth*, as we shall see, she uneasily registers some effects of their conjunction.

If Veblen's hypothesis about the evolution of masculine honor is correct, the timorous Percy Gryce suggests just how far from the world of "predatory exploit" some gentlemanly specimens have come. Once defined by Lily's cousin as "the young man who had promised his mother never to go out in the rain without his overshoes" (I, 2, 18), Percy is nonetheless regarded by the members of Lily's set as a very desirable match – though his personal qualities, or lack of them, are nicely summed up by Judy Trenor's exasperated remark when Lily's campaign to charm him ends in failure: "We could none of us imagine your putting up with him for a moment unless you meant to marry him" (I, 7, 60). Insofar as Lily *does* mean to marry him – and her intentions on that score are quite ambivalent – she presumably thinks of her future husband much as she thinks of Judy's own, as "a mere supernumerary in the costly show for which his money paid" (I, 7, 68). Less coarse than Gus Trenor and – to all appearances, at least – far less aggressive sexually, Percy Gryce chiefly promises to supply the means by which "she would have smarter gowns than Judy Trenor, and far, far more jewels than Bertha Dorset" (I, 4, 41). As Veblen observes when he too considers the dressing of the leisure class, the woman's function is "to put in evidence her household's ability to pay" and thereby to sustain "the good name of the household to which she belongs" (Veblen, 180). And this is precisely what Lily imagines herself doing when she determines to take the place of the Gryce Americana – to be to Percy "the one possession in which he took sufficient pride to spend money on it." Lily "resolved so to identify herself with her husband's vanity," Wharton writes, "that to gratify her wishes would be to him the most exquisite form of self-indulgence" (I, 4, 41), as if the "exquisite" pleasure Percy now feels when he sees his name in print (I, 2, 20) were in the future to be aroused instead by the woman who triumphantly carried that name in public. As Lily's husband, the simultaneously vain and timid Percy could continue to feel himself at once safely hidden and gloriously displayed – even as he felt himself paradoxically "secure in the shelter of her conspicuousness" when she elegantly made tea for him in the public train (I, 2, 18).

Percy Gryce owes his leisure to the fortune he has inherited from his father, a fortune "which the late Mr. Gryce had made," Wharton mischievously informs us, "out of a patent device for excluding fresh air from hotels." After the death of Jefferson Gryce, the mother and son leave their native Albany and settle in New York, where Percy dutifully spends his weekdays being "initiated with becoming reverence into every detail of the art of accumulation" by the "batch of pale men on small salaries" who have hitherto managed the Gryce estate (I, 2, 21). By the standards of the Old World, this is very new money indeed, but in comparison to most of the wealthy men in *The House of Mirth*, Percy Gryce possesses a hallowed claim to the status of gentleman. Though Veblen technically distinguishes between the middle classes, where men work hard so that their wives can vicariously perform their leisure for them, and the leisure class proper, where both sexes conspicuously abstain from productive labor, the world of *The House of Mirth* is largely a world of women. It is they who produce the "impressions" by which social ascent is finally measured – as Lily implicitly recognizes when she regrets not having purchased Rosedale's silence after their awkward encounter by allowing herself to be seen with him at the train station, or when she later tries to appease him by taking a "conspicuous" walk with him at the Van Osburgh wedding (I, 8, 77). And as Rosedale himself will in turn come to recognize, the subtleties and refinement of a woman like Lily – her very superiority to "mere display" (I, 4, 34) – only intensify the worth of such occasions. "He had his race's accuracy in the appraisal of values," the narrator comments of Rosedale, after Lily snubs him in front of Selden's apartment, "and to be seen walking down the platform at the crowded afternoon hour in the company of Miss Lily Bart would have been money in his pocket, as he might himself have phrased it" (I, 2, 15). As Veblen would have predicted, however, the refinement of Rosedale's own powers of discrimination keeps pace with his social progress; and neither his view of Lily, nor our view of him, will be quite this crude by the novel's end. Rosedale's feeling for "shades of difference" (I, 11, 96) may never quite match Lily's "affinity to all the subtler manifestations of wealth" (I, 4, 34), but he knows full well when he proposes to her that "it's only the showy things that are cheap" (I, 15, 140); and by their final encounter he will even have come to admire her "scruples and resistances" as much as her "delicacy of feature" and "fastidiousness of manner" – "as though he were a collector who had learned to distinguish minor differences of design and quality in some long-coveted object" (II, 11, 234).[8]

Though Lily does not finally find a "collector" either in Gryce or in Rosedale, the novel repeatedly emphasizes that she has no other function, that the position of leisure-class marker is the only one she knows how to fill. "Since she had been brought up to be ornamental, she could hardly blame herself for failing to serve any practical purpose," the narrator remarks when Lily later tries and fails to earn her living as a milliner. "It was bitter to acknowledge her inferiority even to herself, but the fact had been brought home to her that as a breadwinner she could never compete with professional ability" (II, 11, 232). Yet as Veblen likes to remind us by frequently comparing the leisure-class wife and the liveried servant, the painstaking display of uselessness for which such a woman has been raised is itself a kind of job, an elaborate "performance" on behalf of another. Neither a gentleman's wife nor his footman, for instance, is principally engaged in productive labor, but both are "dependents who perform vicarious leisure for him," and both may devote considerable time and effort to the task of display for which they have been hired. "The leisure of the servant is not his own leisure," Veblen remarks, but "a specialised service directed to the furtherance of his master's fulness of life"; and "so long as the household with a male head remains in force," the wife too "is still primarily a servant," one who "should not only perform certain offices" but demonstrate "the effects of special training and practice in subservience" (Veblen, 80, 60). While Wharton occasionally writes as if women like Lily were trained to be altogether incapable of work – the language of such passages merely reflecting the familiar identification of "work" with openly paid employment – the novel as a whole clearly shares Veblen's perception.[9] As a hanger-on in the households of her wealthy friends, practiced in the minor forms of "social drudgery" and accustomed to be "in bondage to other people's pleasure," Lily is perpetually in training for the role she never assumes; and "in her bitter moods," the narrator observes, "it sometimes struck her that she and her maid were in the same position, except that the latter received her wages more regularly" (I, 3, 24). When Lily does briefly work for regular wages at Mme. Regina's, she deliberately chooses to engage in productive labor, hoping to learn the trade of hat making and avoid having to accept the modeling job the proprietor would have preferred to offer her. Though Lily's "charming listless hands" prove useless at the task, we have no reason to question the soundness of Mme. Regina's original judgment: "As a displayer of hats, a fashionable beauty might be a valuable asset" (II, 10, 221, 222).

Tending as it does to make her own person the principal object of her labor, a woman's conspicuous display of herself is nonetheless work of a very peculiar kind – a fact to which Wharton is understandably more sensitive than Veblen. The theorist of the leisure class knows quite well that he lives in a "patriarchal régime" which still treats a woman as her husband's "chattel," and he is particularly shrewd about the way in which her dress serves to emphasize the fact by obviously disabling her from any independent activity: "The high heel, the skirt, the impracticable bonnet, the corset, and the general disregard of the wearer's comfort which is an obvious feature of all civilised women's apparel," Veblen characteristically remarks, "are so many items of evidence to the effect that in the modern civilised scheme of life the woman is still, in theory, the economic dependent of the man" (Veblen, 70, 71, 181–2). Concerned as he is with woman's conspicuous uselessness, however, Veblen scarcely seems to notice how the cult of her physical beauty contributes to her status as an object, or to remark that the more attractive a woman, the greater her value as a vehicle of display.

Apart from complaining to Selden that "we are expected to be pretty and well-dressed till we drop" (I, 1, 12), Lily herself never seems to register any particular discomfort regarding her clothes, though Selden, watching her pour tea in his apartment, imagines "the links of her bracelet . . . like manacles chaining her to her fate" and her hand itself significantly "polished as a bit of old ivory" (I, 1, 8). After Lily alludes jokingly to a potential mother-in-law's fear that she might have had "all the family jewels reset," he notes "with a purely impersonal enjoyment, how evenly the black lashes were set in her smooth white lids" (I, 1, 10). Earlier, when they first set out on the walk from Grand Central Station, he had "a confused sense that she must have cost a great deal to make" (I, 1, 7). Nor, of course, is Selden the only one who thus confuses the beautiful woman with a valuable crafted object. "If I want a thing I'm willing to pay," Rosedale announces when he proposes to Lily: "I don't go up to the counter, and then wonder if the article's worth the price." After Mr. Bart's bankruptcy and death, Mrs. Bart thought of Lily's beauty as "the last asset in their fortunes" and "watched it jealously, as though it were her own property and Lily its mere custodian" (I, 3, 29). But we hardly need the particular facts of her family history to explain how Lily too comes to think of her beauty as an impersonal thing: as feminist critics have been quick to observe, such objectification of woman's beauty only exaggerates the values of the culture.[10] "Her beauty itself was not the mere ephemeral possession it might have been in the hands of inexperience," Wharton writes; "her skill in enhancing it, the care she took of it, the use she made of it, seemed to give it a kind of permanence. She felt she could trust it to carry her through to the end" (I, 4, 41). Like Lily's obsessive mirror gazing, the sort of alienation registered by these impersonal pronouns is so familiar as almost to pass without notice – as is the way in which the beautiful heroine serves the novelist both as wish fulfillment and moralistic warning. But if Lily's trust in her beauty is meant to be unfounded, her appraisal of what she has to display is all too accurate. Lily "fails" on the marriage market because she finally resists the impulse to sell herself, not because she judges the values of that market inaccurately.[11]

As we have already seen, the New York of this novel proves in one sense terrifyingly limited – a world so narrow and intimate that Lily can scarcely take a step without encountering someone she knows. But *The House of Mirth* also represents a leisure class in the process of rapid expansion, and anxiously foresees how its opportunities for display will be many times magnified by the instruments of modern publicity. When Wharton imagines her characters displaying themselves, she thinks of newspapers and fashion journals, "a blaze of electric light," photographs in the "Sunday Supplements" (II, 9, 213, 214) – and even the motion picture camera ready to roll at the Van Osburgh wedding:

It was the "simple country wedding" to which guests are conveyed in special trains, and from which the hordes of the uninvited have to be fended off by the intervention of the police. While these sylvan rites were taking place, in a church packed with fashion and festooned with orchids, the representatives of the press were threading their way, notebook in hand, through the labyrinth of wedding presents, and the agent of a cinematograph syndicate was setting up his apparatus at the church door. It was the kind of scene in which Lily had often pictured herself as taking the principal part, and on this occasion the fact that she was once more merely a casual spectator, instead of the mystically veiled figure occupying the centre of attention, strengthened her resolve to assume the latter part before the year was over. (I, 8, 69)

The line that separates a bride from a silent film star seems thin indeed; and though Lily never does get the part, she will later discover that she nonetheless had her fans. "I used to watch for your name in the papers, and we'd talk over what you were doing, and read the descriptions of the dresses you wore," Nettie Struther declares, explaining how she named her baby "Marry Anto'nette" because the actress who played the doomed queen reminded her of Lily (II, 13, 244). Listening to the casual chatter with which her fellow workers at Mme. Regina's pass the time, Lily has already learned something of how the city's less conspicuous inhabitants follow the lives of the rich and the famous:

On and on it flowed, a current of meaningless sound, on which, startlingly enough, a familiar name now and then floated to the surface. It was the strangest part of Lily's strange experience, the hearing of these names, the seeing the fragmentary and distorted image of the world she had lived in reflected in the mirror of the working-girls' minds. She had never before suspected the mixture of insatiable curiosity and contemptuous freedom with which she and her kind were discussed in this underworld of toilers who lived on their vanity and self-indulgence. Every girl in Mme. Regina's work-room knew to whom the headgear in her hands was destined, and had her opinion of its future wearer, and a definite knowledge of the latter's place in the social system. That Lily was a star fallen from that sky did not, after the first stir of curiosity had subsided, materially add to their interest in her. She had fallen, she had "gone under," and true to the ideal of their race, they were awed only by success – by the gross tangible image of material achievement. (II, 10, 223)

Though their measure of success remains that of conspicuous consumption ("the gross tangible image of material achievement"), these workers discuss the women of the leisure class with the same casual avidity with which we gossip about movie stars and rock musicians; and as in our case, the thrill of the gossip derives from a peculiar mixture of distance and intimacy. Compared to a modern fan, who typically "knows" her celebrities only through the media, an employee at Mme. Regina's has a relatively direct relation to the objects of her curiosity: she still makes hats with her own hands, after all, for the heads of those she talks about. But Wharton also emphasizes that those who circulate in the "social system" know nothing of the "underworld" that observes them, while only the glorious remoteness of the leisured heavens catches the attention of the workers: the fallen star has no power to interest them.

Despite the presence of the cinematographer at the Van Osburgh wedding, *The House of Mirth* can only anticipate the possibilities of modern publicity: if Lily is a kind of star, her most triumphant performance still takes the form of a *tableau vivant* at a private house party, and the painting she chooses to recreate is an elegantly simple eighteenth-century portrait. But since the Brys hope "to attack society collectively" by putting on "a general entertainment," and since their newly constructed mansion has rooms "immense" enough to accommodate a "throng," the distinction between private and public life is not very great (I, 12, 103, 104). Indeed, even before the *tableaux* begin, Wharton suggests, the Brys' domestic interior can scarcely be distinguished from a stage set: "So recent, so rapidly-evoked was the whole *mise-en-scène* that one had to touch the marble columns to learn they were not of cardboard, to seat one's self in one of the damask-and-gold arm-chairs to be sure it was not painted against the wall" (I, 12, 104). At once a kind of dramatic performance and a sequence of static, museumlike displays, the *tableaux vivants* merely exaggerate the ordinary forms of leisure-class life; and Lily, as we might expect, "was in her element on such occasions" (I, 12, 103). Simply clothed in the pale and flowing draperies of the Reynolds portrait, she does not so much transcend the world of conspicuous display as show off her superior refinement – a fitting emblem of the "spiritualisation of the scheme of symbolism in dress" which Veblen identifies with the highest reaches of the pecuniary culture.[12] "In that plain white dress," the newly discriminating Rosedale later tells her, she looked as if she "had a crown on" (I, 15, 140). In that dress she also exhibits her own figure to best advantage – as the cruder comments of "that experienced connoisseur," Ned Van Alstyne, clearly register: "What's a woman want with jewels when she's got herself to show? The trouble is that all these fal-bals they wear cover up their figures when they've got 'em. I never knew till tonight what an outline Lily has" (I, 13, 106, 109). Like the actress who manages to represent an imaginary character even as she reminds the viewer all the more intensely of her own identity, Lily paradoxically succeeds as Reynolds's "Mrs. Lloyd" by giving the audience "a picture which was simply and undisguisedly the portrait of Miss Bart." In the other *tableaux*, the narrator observes, "the personality of the actors [had] been subdued to the scenes they figured in," but "here there could be no mistaking the predominance of personality. . . . She had shown her artistic intelligence in selecting a type so like her own that she could embody the person represented without ceasing to be herself" (I, 12, 106). When Gerty Farish innocently observes of the Reynolds costume that "it makes her look *like* the real Lily" (I, 12, 107; emphasis added), she unwittingly sums up the difficulties of locating depths in this world of appearances, a world in which the "real" self keeps threatening to prove just another conspicuous performance.

In a still more nightmarish version of the novel's opening sequence, Lily's triumphant self-display quickly yields to a more threatening scene of observation, when Gus Trenor tricks her into visiting him alone the following evening. Long chafing at Lily's failure to return any sexual favors for the money he has advanced (it turns out he has invested *in* her rather than for her), Trenor is driven to proprietary outrage by the very spectacle of her public exhibition: "I went to that damned vulgar party just to see you," he drunkenly complains, "and there was everybody talking about you, and asking me if I'd ever seen anything so stunning, and when I tried to come up and say a word, you never took any notice, but just went on laughing and joking with a lot of asses who only wanted to be able to swagger about afterward, and look knowing when you were mentioned" (I, 13, 112). Significantly, that which certifies Lily's value as conspicuous waste only increases her vulnerability; and Trenor's assault is checked not by "her helpless useless hands" but by the timely intervention of a figurative "hand of inherited order" that "plucked back the bewildered mind which passion had jolted from its ruts" (I, 12, 117). Yet if this attempted rape is the most obvious and brutal consequence of her glorious display the previous evening, Selden's glimpse of her as she leaves the Trenor house proves more insidiously devastating.[13] Though she physically manages to elude Trenor's grasp, she does not escape the imputations of having been seen in his presence, nor does she ever know that she needs to defend herself from this more insidious assault, which is so much more typical of the novel. Indeed, Wharton intensifies the painfulness of the episode by giving it to us twice, once from Lily's point of view, as she confronts Trenor and then flees in misery to Gerty Farish, and again from Selden's, as he walks with Ned Van Alstyne late at night down Fifth Avenue:

The walking-stick which Van Alstyne swung . . . dropped to a startled "Hallo!" as the door opened and two figures were seen silhouetted against the hall-light. At the same moment a hansom halted at the curb-stone, and one of the figures floated down to it in a haze of evening draperies; while the other, black and bulky, remained persistently projected against the light.

For an immeasurable second the two spectators of the incident were silent; then the house-door closed, the hansom rolled off, and the whole scene slipped by as if with the turn of a stereopticon. (I, 14, 127)

As when she left Selden's apartment and encountered Rosedale, Lily seems unable to step out into the street without being recognized – only this time it is Selden who ironically happens by as witness. Both spectators of this silent *tableau* have just heard Jack Stepney complain of her "standing there as if she was up at auction" at the previous evening's performance (I, 14, 124); now they chance upon this second briefly illuminated scene, and "as if with the turn of a stereopticon," it destroys Selden's already fragile faith in Lily. Instead of coming to her rescue the next day with a proposal of marriage, he catches the first boat for Havana. Though he will next appear at Monte Carlo, in the second book of the novel, in time to catch the spectacular crowd scenes whose climax is the dramatic staging of Lily's ostracism, this silent pantomine in New York opens the final rift between them. Only when Selden discovers the check made out to Trenor that Lily leaves behind at her death does he belatedly begin to realize that his interpretation of the scene might be mistaken.

By beginning the novel's second book with a spectacle that produces the effect of a closing *tableau,* Wharton self-consciously calls attention to the way in which the Monte Carlo scenes resemble the grand finale of her heroine's conspicuous career. Several episodes will intervene before Lily's lonely death in a New York boardinghouse, but each only marks a further phase of the social descent that clearly begins with her ignominious expulsion from Bertha's yacht. When Selden arrives at Monte Carlo, the cast has been assembled as for the final crowd scene:

It was mid-April, and one felt that the revelry had reached its climax and that the desultory groups in the square and gardens would soon dissolve and re-form in other scenes. Meanwhile the last moments of the performance seemed to gain an added brightness from the hovering threat of the curtain. The quality of the air, the exuberance of the flowers, the blue intensity of sea and sky, produced the effect of a closing *tableau,* when all the lights are turned on at once. This impression was presently heightened by the way in which a consciously conspicuous group of people advanced to the middle front, and stood before Selden with the air of the chief performers gathered together by the exigencies of the final effect. Their appearance confirmed the impression that the show had been staged regardless of expense, and emphasized its resemblance to one of those "costume-plays" in which the protagonists walk through the passions without displacing a drapery. The ladies stood in unrelated attitudes calculated to isolate their effects, and the men hung about them as irrelevantly as stage heroes whose tailors are named in the programme. (II, 1, 143–4)

The passage suggests a reprise of the New York *tableaux,* except that there is no longer even the pretense of a distinction between the costume play on stage and the costume play off: for the "consciously conspicuous" members of the leisure class, after all, a resort like Monte Carlo exists entirely for show. Not surprisingly, we soon learn that "Lily has been a tremendous success" in these repeat performances (II, 1, 146). But what commences in one kind of conspicuousness for the novel's heroine ends with the other, as Bertha's deliberate timing converts a scene of celebrity into the public staging of a scandal.

Bertha takes care to perform her dramatic gesture in the middle of a fashionable restaurant, a theatrical space "crowded" with people "gathered . . . for the purpose of spectatorship, and accurately posted as to the names and faces of the celebrities they had come to see" (II, 3, 168). And as so often in *The House of Mirth*, a representative of the press is on hand to heighten the "glare of publicity" (II, 3, 168). If *"Town Talk* was full of her this morning," as Jack Stepney complains the day after her performance at the Brys' (I, 14, 124), "Riviera Notes" threatens to be still more ominously full of Lily tomorrow, since "the whole scene had touches of intimacy worth their weight in gold to the watchful pen of Mr. Dabham" (II, 3, 169). In Dabham, the insistent watchfulness of the novel becomes an active predatory force: "His little eyes were like tentacles thrown out to catch the floating intimations with which, to Selden, the air at moments seemed thick."[14] Though the anxious Selden tries to persuade himself that the scene will afford the reporter nothing but "leisure to note the elegance of the ladies' gowns" – the "surprises and subtleties" of Bertha's in particular seem to him to "challenge . . . all the wealth of Mr. Dabham's vocabulary" (II, 3, 168) – Bertha's gown soon proves less subtle and surprising than the woman herself, and the conspicuous waste of her dress fades before her dramatic contribution to the wasting of Lily.

By the time that Lily returns to New York, the scandal has preceded her, and the damage has irretrievably spread. Translating a social cut into a cut in hard currency, Mrs. Peniston's decision to disinherit her niece at once confirms and reproduces Mrs. Dorset's gesture, even as the space that widens about Lily when the other women fall back from her after the reading of the will exaggerates her "slightly isolated position" and the "averted looks" of the women in the earlier scene (II, 3, 169, 170). "The truth about any girl is that once she's talked about she's done for," Lily sums up her situation to Gerty Farish (II, 4, 176) – a rule that suspiciously resembles those "copy-book axioms" she has earlier associated with her aunt and impatiently dismissed as "all meant to apply to conduct in the early fifties" (I, 1, 9–10). Though Lily never specifies which axioms she has in mind, the "truth" she cites is unmistakably one of Mrs. Peniston's: "It was horrible of a young girl to let herself be talked about" (I, 11, 100). But if, as Lily has begun to discover, such old-fashioned axioms

still painfully apply, the real "truth about any girl" is that her
position is impossible to begin with, since the rules in her aunt's
copy-book condemn precisely what the leisure class requires of
its beautiful women. Indeed, books directed at the marriageable
young woman had long taken as axiomatic that she should *not*
be seen and talked about – that "the flagrant affectation of
shining in public," as a *Young Lady's Book of Advice and Instruction*
put it in 1859, could lead only to disaster. "Beauty, by being
patent to the public eye, becomes valueless," according to the
author of this book:

I never knew a man, who would willingly choose for his bosom companion, one who was often perambulating the streets, or exhibiting
herself at public places. . . .
    The attractions of a beautiful woman are sure to suffer, if seen too
frequently; modest reserve, like the distance kept by royal personages,
contributes to maintain the proper reverence. Nothing can be more
impolitic in young ladies, than to make themselves too cheap.[15]

Rather, "that retiring delicacy which avoids the public eye, and
is disconcerted even at the gaze of admiration, is the most
powerful charm of woman," the book suggests on another page.
"It is the safeguard and protection of all feminine virtues, and she
who is under the restraint of modesty, is secure from every evil
tendency."[16] In Mrs. Peniston's youth, such wisdom could have
been found in hundreds of places; and we hardly need imagine
that she read this particular tome of *Advice and Instruction* to
recognize how something very like its assumptions prompts her
outraged reaction to the rumors that involve her niece – or to
recognize how directly such axioms contradict the unstated laws
of leisure-class consumption and display. Notice how, according
to the advice book, the public exhibition of the young lady's
beauty threatens to make her too "cheap" – an economic law that
altogether inverts the theory of values articulated by Veblen. Of
course, the book advised young women still on the market,
whereas Veblen studies the role of those already purchased in
marriage: *The Young Lady's Book* urged a woman to keep herself
scarce in order to drive up her price, while *The Theory of the Leisure
Class* analyzes how she helps men to show off what prices they

can afford to pay. But even conduct books assumed that the marriageable young woman had to "come out" in order to display herself most effectively, and even the more cynical members of the married leisure class, as *The House of Mirth* suggests, were capable of deliberately exploiting the modesty rules for the making of scandal. And if a double bind seizes women most forcibly as they attempt to move from one officially approved state to another, Wharton heightens the tension by imagining a heroine who has already been too long on the market: a *"jeune fille à marier"* of twenty-nine, and shop-worn enough to joke about it, is especially vulnerable (I, 6, 56).

Well before Bertha Dorset accuses Lily of having been "so conspicuously" alone with George Dorset late at night in Monte Carlo (II, 2, 161), Grace Stepney begins to alienate Mrs. Peniston from her niece by passing on rumors that have been circulating about the latter's relation to Gus Trenor. "People always say unpleasant things," she remarks with a complacent sense of her worldly superiority to Mrs. Peniston – "and certainly they're a great deal together," she adds maliciously. "It's a pity Lily makes herself so conspicuous."

> *"Conspicuous!"* gasped Mrs. Peniston. She bent forward, lowering her voice to mitigate the horror. "What sort of things do they say? That he means to get a divorce and marry her?"
> Grace Stepney laughed outright. "Dear me, no! He would hardly do that. It – it's a flirtation – nothing more."
> "A flirtation? Between my niece and a married man?" (I, 11, 98)

Wharton makes clear that this is old New York speaking – and that the closed and comparatively small town of Mrs. Peniston's girlhood is rapidly disappearing into the speed and crowds of the modern city. Significantly enough, Mrs. Peniston never figures in those large throngs of spectators who gaze admiringly on her niece. Indeed, so far as we can tell, she scarcely ever ventures beyond her drawing room, where she keeps her imagination as "shrouded," the narrator suggests, as the furniture (I, 11, 98). Yet Mrs. Peniston too, of course, is a watcher – a "looker-on at life" whose mind has earlier been figured as "one of those little mirrors which her Dutch ancestors were accustomed to affix to their upper windows, so that from the depths of an impenetrable domesticity they might see what was happening in the street" (I, 3, 32). Her New York has no rush hours at Grand Central Station, in other words, just those villagelike streets into which her niece keeps stepping at awkward moments, streets whose only occupant proves always, however implausibly, someone she knows. Caught between the imperative to display herself and the injunction to keep herself modestly out of sight, Lily dies, one might say, partly because she lives in both Veblen's city and Mrs. Peniston's.[17]

In the later chapters of *The House of Mirth*, and in occasional retrospective remarks on the novel to others, Wharton sometimes evokes its old New York with a certain incongruous nostalgia – as if by comparison to the spectacularly vulgar standards of the newest nouveaux riches, Mrs. Peniston's copy-book axioms had suddenly been converted into satisfactory guides to the moral life. "Compared with the vast gilded void of Mrs. Hatch's existence," for example, "the life of Lily's former friends seemed packed with ordered activities." Confronted with the multiply divorced and very wealthy Mrs. Hatch, who arrives from somewhere vaguely out west to swim "in a haze of indeterminate enthusiasms, of aspirations culled from the stage, the newspapers, the fashion-journals, and a gaudy world of sport," Lily suddenly discovers that "even the most irresponsible pretty woman of her acquaintance had her inherited obligations, her conventional benevolences, her share in the working of the great civic machine; and all hung together in the solidarity of these traditional functions" (II, 9, 215). In an often-quoted valedictory passage, the narrator deplores Lily's "rootless and ephemeral" life, her lack of "grave endearing traditions" and a "centre of early pieties," implicitly comparing the House of Mirth to "the concrete image of the old house stored with visual memories, or . . . the conception of the house not built with hands, but made up of inherited passions and loyalties" (II, 13, 248). Writing about the novel to the rector of New York's Trinity Church a few months after it was published, Wharton similarly appeared to suggest that her subject was the difference between the traditional loyalties of the old money and the rootlessness of the new: "Social conditions as they are just now in our new world, where the sudden possession of money has come without inherited obligations, or any traditional sense of solidarity between the classes, is a vast & absorbing field for the novelist."[18] At such moments it is almost as if Wharton wanted to forget the collusion of old money and new that she had in fact represented, or as if she could somehow undo her heroine's fate by substituting a consoling image of the past for the world of "inherited obligations" she had already satirized in Mrs. Peniston.

The most vivid thing about her was the fact that her grandmother had been a Van Alstyne. This connection with the well-fed and industrious stock of early New York revealed itself in the glacial neatness of Mrs. Peniston's drawing-room and in the excellence of her cuisine. She belonged to the class of old New Yorkers who have always lived well, dressed expensively, and done little else; and to these inherited obligations Mrs. Peniston faithfully conformed. (I, 3, 32)

Wharton sometimes writes as if "the sudden possession of money" marked a great divide between this old world and the new, but she knows as well as Veblen himself did that the leisure class is an archaic institution. Mrs. Peniston might register shock at Mrs. Dorset's gambling, not to mention her adulteries, but both women recognize an obligation to live well and dress expensively; and from beyond the grave, as we have seen, the older woman reenacts the younger one's cut of Lily.

Wharton similarly confuses an older world with the new in a letter of the same year, even as she protests to her Bostonian correspondent against the suggestion that she has "'stripped' New York society" in her novel:

New York society is still amply clad, & the little corner of its garment that I lifted was meant to show only that little atrophied organ – the group of idle & dull people – that exists in any big & wealthy social body. If it seems more conspicuous in New York than in an old civilization, it is because the whole social organization with us is so much smaller & less elaborate – & if, as I believe, it is more harmful in its influence, it is because fewer responsibilities attach to money with us than in other societies.

How a "little atrophied organ" could seem "conspicuous" – even after the novelist has metaphorically lifted a corner of a garment to reveal it – is simply not clear, unless she is actually so bold as to mean the male genitals of New York. Indeed, this uneasy figure makes it impossible to decide what class of people she professes to have indicted. Though Wharton could well argue that a parvenu like Norma Hatch only seems conspicuous because New York is a comparatively small and uncomplicated civilization, the group of "idle & dull people" seems rather to evoke Mrs. Peniston's set – and so, of course, do the suggestions of age and sexual withering in "that little atrophied organ." In the letter as elsewhere, what does seem clear is the writer's anxiety to distance herself from the aggressive implications of her own satire. "Forgive this long discourse," she continues, "but you see I had to come to the defense of my own town, which, I assure you, has many mansions outside of the little House of Mirth."[19] There are "many mansions," however, in *The House of Mirth*, and little suggestion of any "society" outside them. Between the oppressive darkness of Mrs. Peniston's drawing room – the past of Wharton's memory, it is tempting to suggest, rather than of her pious wishes – and the vulgar glare of a place like the Emporium Hotel, where the notorious Mrs. Hatch takes up residence, the novel does not really offer its heroine anything to choose.[20]

In *The House of Mirth*, it often seems, everyone is a "looker-on" and only appearances count.[21] As Simon Rosedale rather brutally makes clear when he declines to renew his marriage proposal to Lily, what matters is not the truth about Lily, but how she looks to others. "If they are not true," Lily asks of the stories that have been circulating about her, "doesn't *that* alter the situation?" "I believe it does in novels," Rosedale steadily replies, "but I'm certain it don't in real life" (II, 7, 199, 200). Like so many novelists, Wharton professes to give us not fiction but "real life" – and with the further paradox that reality in *The House of Mirth* is highly artificial. The brutal truth she emphasizes is that Lily lives in a world of stage sets and mirrors, where even false stories can kill.[22] But like any novelist who professes to give us "real life," Wharton also takes advantage of the possibilities of fiction: insisting that in Lily Bart's world only appearances count, she nonetheless offers us an interior view, the privileged access to another's consciousness that only fiction can provide. Unlike all those who watch Lily Bart, we alone know, for example, that she chooses to burn Bertha's letters rather than to use them; and for us, at least, such knowledge does make a difference. That difference should not be exaggerated: what the novel actually gives us through its heroine is not an alternative vision, just the faltering pulse of resistance, which the novelist and reader register to the bitter end. Consciousness in *The House of Mirth* primarily defines itself by negating the world of appearances.

NOTES

1. This essay originally appeared in *ELH* 59 (1992): 713–34. Permission to reprint is gratefully acknowledged.

2. For a related discussion of Lily's resistance to being watched as she burns Bertha's letters, see Barbara Hochman, "The Rewards of Representation: Edith Wharton, Lily Bart and the Writer/ Reader Interchange," *Novel* 24 (1991): 157–8. Hochman interprets Lily's covert gesture in this scene as a defiant renunciation of the audience on which her existence has hitherto depended and as a sign of Wharton's own ambivalent relation to her readers. Though Hochman also calls the burning of the letters "an affirmation of the luxurious wastefulness [Lily] has always longed to indulge" (157), the very inconspicuousness of the gesture disqualifies it as an act of wasting in the Veblenesque sense elaborated here.

3. To the best of my knowledge, Wharton never specifically mentions having read *The Theory of the Leisure Class*, but, as we shall see, the evidence of *The House of Mirth* strongly suggests that she was familiar with its arguments and its vocabulary. For some other uses of Veblen to illuminate the novel, see Elizabeth Ammons, *Edith Wharton's Argument with America* (Athens: University of Georgia Press, 1980), 28–31; Amy Kaplan, "Edith Wharton's Profession of Authorship," *ELH* 53 (1986): 434–5; Sandra M. Gilbert and Susan Gubar, *No Man's Land: The Place of the Woman Writer in the Twentieth Century, Vol. II: Sexchanges* (New Haven: Yale University Press, 1989), 130–1, 137–9, 143–4; and, briefly, Cynthia Griffin Wolff's introduction to Edith Wharton, *The House of Mirth* (Harmondsworth: Penguin, 1985), xxi–xxii.

4. Edith Wharton, *A Backward Glance* (New York: Appleton, 1934), 207.

5. Thorstein Veblen, *The Theory of the Leisure Class: An Economic Study of Institutions* (New York: Modern Library, 1934), 87. All subsequent references in the text are to this edition.

6. Veblen, 180. As a number of critics have observed, an earlier title for *The House of Mirth* was "A Moment's Ornament." See R. W. B. Lewis, *Edith Wharton: A Biography* (New York: Harper & Row, 1975), 109.

7. Veblen, 34. "Complacency" is another key word in Veblen's vocabulary; compare (among numerous other instances) the phrase "in order . . . to retain one's self-complacency" quoted earlier. Though Wharton does not ring as many changes on the word as she does on "conspicuous," she again uses it in Veblen's sense when Lily tries to reassure an anxious Judy Trenor that her renown as a hostess will not suffer from invidious comparisons to Maria Van Osburgh. "You know perfectly well that, if Mrs. Van Osburgh were to get all the right people and leave you with all the wrong ones, you'd manage to make things go off, and she wouldn't," Lily protests – on which the narrator comments: "Such an assurance would usually have restored Mrs. Trenor's complacency; but on this occasion it did not chase the cloud from her brow" (I, 4, 36). Compare also the satisfaction Lily takes in the attentions of the relatively vulgar Wellington Brys after the failure of her campaign for Percy Gryce: "Mrs. Bry's admiration was a mirror in which Lily's self-complacency recovered its lost outline. . . . If these people paid court to her it proved that she was still conspicuous in the world to which they aspired" (I, 10, 88–9).

8. Compare Veblen's similar observation about the refinement of taste that develops when a sufficiently large number of people have "the leisure for acquiring skill in interpreting the subtler signs of expenditure" (187).

9. Compare to Ammons, 30–3.

10. On Lily's relation to herself as a beautiful object, see especially Judith Fetterley, " 'The Temptation to be a Beautiful Object': Double Standard and Double Bind in *The House of Mirth*," *Studies in American Fiction* 5 (1977): 199–211; and Cynthia Griffin Wolff, *A Feast of Words: The Triumph of Edith Wharton* (New York: Oxford, 1978), 112–33.

11. For a very different view of Lily's relation to the market, see Walter Benn Michaels, *The Gold Standard and the Logic of Naturalism* (Berke-

ley: University of California Press, 1987), 228–34. In Michaels's account, Lily most closely shares the values of the market when she most appears to oppose them – when she refuses Rosedale's suggestion that she blackmail Bertha and marry him, for example, or even when she decides to swallow the dose of chloral that finally destroys her. What such acts have in common is Lily's deliberate assumption of risk, a "passion for gambling," Michaels contends, that "is an expression of her passion for the market" (230) and by implication, at least, of the novelist's own values as well. While his reading brilliantly evokes the attractions of indeterminacy for Lily and Wharton alike (Lily is most "interesting" to herself when she doesn't quite know what she's up to), it is less effective in explaining why the novel consistently associates such risk taking with self-destruction. The argument advanced here is closer to that of Wai-Chee Dimock, "Debasing Exchange: Edith Wharton's *The House of Mirth*," *PMLA* 100 (1985): 783–91. Dimock sees the burning of the letters as a gesture of resistance to the exchange system, even as she makes clear how the novel renders all such gestures futile.

12. Veblen, 187. As the leisure class develops, in Veblen's words, "the method of advertisement undergoes a refinement," and "'loud' dress becomes offensive to people of taste, as evincing an undue desire to reach and impress the untrained sensibilities of the vulgar."

13. See Kaplan, "Edith Wharton's Profession": "It is no accident that Trenor's attempted rape in the privacy of an empty drawing room follows this scene [the Bry *tableaux*], collapsing the line between public display of the self as art and the private vulnerability of the lady at home" (449).

14. Though in this passage it seems scarcely possible – or necessary – to distinguish Selden's view of Dabham from Wharton's, I would not like to suggest that we should regularly identify the hero's viewpoint with that of the novel as a whole. Indeed, despite Selden's subsequent desire to "grip Dabham by the collar and fling him out into the street," the cynical watchfulness of the novel's hero has all too much in common with that of the gossip columnist. Note, for example, how Selden immediately begins to speculate about what "weakness" of Lily's has prompted this scene, as his "reason obstinately harped on the proverbial relation between smoke and fire" (II, 3, 169, 170).

15. *The Young Lady's Book of Advice and Instruction* (Glasgow and London: W. R. M'Phun, 1859), 30, 28–9.

16. *The Young Lady's Book,* 11–12. According to this work, "the chief ornament of the female character is modesty" (11) – a commonplace formula worth comparing to Wharton's satiric allusion to the marriageable young woman as "a moment's ornament" (see note 6). For a more extensive treatment of the double binds implicit in such rhetoric, see my *Fictions of Modesty: Women and Courtship in the English Novel* (Chicago: University of Chicago Press, 1991).

17. When Diana Trilling writes of "Mrs. Wharton's, and Lily's, society," that "their New York is very much a small town where everyone knows everyone else and where the boundaries even upon one's physical movements are rigidly prescribed," she clearly has Mrs. Peniston in mind; indeed, she goes on to assert that Lily's aunt "can sit at her window and be as well-informed of the comings and goings of her acquaintances as if she were still young and active," though this rather literalizes Wharton's metaphor. But Mrs. Peniston's New York is not – or not simply, at least – Lily's and Wharton's: as I have tried to show, theirs is also the Veblenesque city of conspicuous consumption. Trilling shrewdly remarks Lily's "inability to evade the eyes of the world and lose herself in the crowd," but fails to register what Wharton knows all too well: how much Lily's culture simultaneously encourages her to court the eyes she would evade. See *"The House of Mirth* Revisited," in *Edith Wharton: A Collection of Critical Essays,* ed. Irving Howe (Englewood Cliffs, N.J.: Prentice-Hall, 1962), 115.

18. To Dr. Morgan Dix, December 5 [1905], in *The Letters of Edith Wharton,* ed. R. W. B. Lewis and Nancy Lewis (London: Simon and Schuster, 1988), 99.

19. To William Roscoe Thayer, November 11 [1905], in Wharton, *Letters,* 96–7.

20. For a related account of how Wharton's "essentially aristocratic critique" of the marketplace cannot sustain itself, see Dimock: "And yet, even as she articulates her ideal, she sees that it does not exist, and indeed has never existed, either in her own experience or in Lily's" (790).

21. See also Nancy Topping Bazin, "The Destruction of Lily Bart: Capitalism, Christianity, and Male Chauvinism," *Denver Quarterly* 17 (1983): 98. "Even more ironic," Bazin remarks of Lily's relation to her "frivolous" society, "is the fact that she is eventually excluded from that world for appearing to do what married women in that milieu actually did with impunity – namely, have affairs and borrow money." This criticism is undoubtedly just, though Lily's temptation

to blackmail suggests that even the impunity of a Bertha Dorset was drastically limited, and that married women too depended on a precarious manipulation of appearances.

22. See Patricia Meyer Spacks, *Gossip* (Chicago: University of Chicago Press, 1986), 173–81.

3

Determining Influences: Resistance and Mentorship in *The House of Mirth* and the Anglo-American Realist Tradition

MARY NYQUIST

Where did he learn so thoroughly to understand the persevereness of a female heart?

> Charlotte Grandison of Sir Charles in *Sir Charles Grandison* (1753–54)[1]

The world had made him extravagant and vain – Extravagance and vanity had made him cold-hearted and selfish. . . . Each faulty propensity in leading him to evil, had led him likewise to punishment.

> Eleanor Dashwood, speaking of Willoughby, in *Sense and Sensibility* (1811)[2]

1

Would Edith Wharton so often be regarded as an imitator of Henry James had she not known him personally? That James was well established when he and Wharton met certainly played a part in positioning him as Wharton's mentor.[3] Unambiguously *literary* signs of special influence are rarely, however, at issue, which makes it difficult not to suspect that Wharton's secondariness is largely a product of gender-based assumptions. Wharton herself was aware that gender is not a neutral factor on the literary scene. But in *The Writing of Fiction*, where she discusses the creative process as a professional writer, she proceeds, impersonally, as if it were. From a feminist perspective, what is most striking about this work is its total lack of interest in female authorship. In the first chapter, "In General," Madame de La Fayette is given credit for having initiated modern fiction in the seventeenth century with *La Princesse de Clèves*. But this introductory chapter doesn't invoke a single other female author, while the following male writers are mentioned at least once: Abbé Prévost, Diderot, Balzac, Dostoievsky, Lesage, Defoe, Fielding, Smollett, Richardson, Scott, Stendhal, Racine, Goethe, Zola, the Goncourts, Feydeau, Flaubert, Thackeray, Tolstoi, Matthew Arnold, Kipling, Mérimée, Maupassant, Conrad, and Proust![4] Eventually, Wharton gives Jane Austen and George Eliot due recognition, and mentions Charlotte Brontë. But the impression Wharton creates in this work is that the writing of fiction is an activity engaged in primarily by brilliant men, among whom must be numbered the gifted Henry James.

Emma appears three times in *The Writing of Fiction*. Wharton refers a few times to Eliot's *Middlemarch*, once to *The Mill on the Floss*, but not at all to *Daniel Deronda*. The latter is known to have been of importance to James, who wrote a review the year it was published, 1876, and whose *The Portrait of a Lady* (1880–81) has long been regarded as influenced by it. More recently, attention has been drawn to a number of interesting interrelations between *Daniel Deronda* and *The House of Mirth* (1905).[5] So far no one has gone the next step, to compare the signs of kinship with *Deronda* to be found in James's *Portrait* and Wharton's *The House of Mirth*. This is not the task I've set myself here, though. *The House of Mirth* stands in complex relation to *Deronda*, since it is mediated, intertextually, by James's *Portrait*. Yet I hope to situate this mediated relationship in an even more intertextually layered context. For *The House of Mirth* is also related through *Deronda* to a series of bourgeois realist novels that pair an influential male mentor with a heroine who badly needs his counsel, whether she's willing to admit it or not. As I hope to show, within this series a significant number of concerns and strategies are shared by *The House of Mirth*, *Daniel Deronda*, and *Emma* (1816), even though the Atlantic, and nearly a century, separate Wharton's novel from Austen's.

Ralph Touchett may be Isabel Archer's mentor, but James's *Portrait* doesn't really belong to this subset. For one thing, unlike his fellow mentors, Touchett is not presented as a potential suitor or even a desirable one. He is repeatedly described as "ugly"; is in addition consumptive, to the point of being an invalid when the novel opens and dead at its close; and is, to boot, Isabel's cousin, cousinship explicitly serving as a tangible obstacle to marriage. Something like romantic interest seems to be felt by Touchett, but in so sublimated a form as to be passion's cousin at third remove. To further diminish Touchett's importance as a lover, James provides Isabel not only with a husband but also with two presentable suitors, both of whom pursue Isabel even after she marries. This severing of mentorship from romance, however, only partly accounts for *Portrait*'s difference from the other novels to be considered here. Romantic interest is definitely a part of, but also a kind of mask for, the intensely charged character of the relationship between heroine and mentor in *Emma, Daniel Deronda*, and *The House of Mirth*. Even more than romance, what is absent in James's *Portrait* are the passionate, often conflictual scenes in which mentor and wayward heroine confront one another. James has refined and displaced the relationship between heroine and mentor so that it no longer holds center stage. But it also no longer holds the heroine under the same compelling, almost hypnotic, spell. What seldom appear in *Portrait* are the moments of barely suppressed longing, of erotic or spiritual yearning, of ambiguously felt relations – swerving, briefly, into intimacy – that so often occur in *Daniel Deronda* and *The House of Mirth*.

Though this is gradually changing, mentorship tends to be a male prerogative in Euro-American, capitalist-patriarchal societies. While female mentorship in the domestic sphere usually goes without recognition, both workplace and marketplace have been populated by far more male than female mentors. Further, the role was one that, until fairly recently, "white" bourgeois husbands were expected to play. In the ideology relating to marriage elaborated in the early modern period, the husband, by virtue of his superior powers, was expected to guide and instruct his wife. As the division between productive and domestic spheres developed, so did the notion that in matters of the heart women are dependent on male initiatives. Male mentorship came to be required in romantic as well as religious, moral, and intellectual pursuits. The past tense may be rather misleading, however. For the notion that "white" female (hetero)sexuality can't know itself except through the active, predatory sexuality of males is alive and well in contemporary mass-produced romance novels, where young (and, increasingly, not-so-young) heroines are represented as coming to self-knowledge through the intervention of a sexualized male figure. Male mentorship – touching numerous areas of the heroine's experience – is a standard feature of mass-produced romance, where the heroine is often infantalized, all the better to see her lover's power. As has often been pointed out, in these texts the heroine's attempts to resist domination almost always turn the hero on. Being encoded as a rejection of her own femininity, her resistance is in any case destined to be overcome. If all else fails, the hero's ability to provide safety will weaken the heroine's determination to resist. Like the giving of advice, the offering of protection always awakens desire, though an unusually resistant heroine may have to be rescued three or four times before she can eroticize her own domination.

In her influential study, Janice Radway suggests that the act of reading popular romance provides women with vicarious satisfaction of a deep, unarticulated need for love and nurturance.[6] Through a process of identification with the heroine, Radway argues, the male protagonist's sharply focused attentions satisfy the female reader's unmet needs, in addition to providing an ecstatic shattering of boundaries that returns her, symbolically, to the pre-Oedipal mother. Like most works of romantic fiction, the novels in the bourgeois realist mentor tradition – novels in which a male mentor plays a significant role – portray mothers who are either absent from the scene of action (through circumstance or death) or else seriously ineffectual as guides. With mothers gone or virtually useless (in the case of Austen's novels, even the surrogate mother isn't able to do her job), the male mentor steps in to fill, as it were, a maternal vacuum. No self-respecting mentor in the realist tradition would behave like the inexplicably indifferent or menacing hero of popular romance (*Jane Eyre*'s Byronic Rochester can, but that's another story). Even more persuasively, then, does his power seem to come from his assuming, as a man, a maternal role.

The mentor's responsive, nurturant qualities are made more attractive by the presence of crudely masculine figures, such as

Sir Hargrave in *Sir Charles Grandison*, John Thrope in *Northanger Abbey*, and Gus Trenor in *Mirth*. His maternal function is performed most successfully by Daniel Deronda, whose receptivity and capacity for sympathetic response are explicitly marked "feminine." Commenting on this, Gillian Beer cites a passage from the Kabbalah noted by George Eliot while working on *Deronda*. If a soul is weakened by the process of becoming earthbound, a process involving the loss of an original androgyny and a differentiation into female and male, it's said that it can be given assistance: "In that case she chooses a companion soul of better fortune or more strength. The stronger of the two then becomes as it were the mother; she carries the sickly one in her bosom and nurses her as a woman her child."[7] In Eliot's novel Deronda clearly plays the strong, nursing mother to the sickly, resistant Gwendolyn. Deronda is said to be in the position of a "mentor" not only to Gwendolyn but also to Hans Meyrik, for whom Deronda has "a brotherly anxiety." Even Deronda's brotherliness, though, is figuratively maternal: "Such friendship easily becomes tender: the one spreads strong sheltering wings that delight in spreading, the other gets the warm protection which is also a delight."[8] In his review, cast in the form of a three-way conversation among recent readers of *Deronda*, James has Theodora, the high-minded, ardent admirer of George Eliot, say, "And as for Deronda himself, I freely confess that I am consumed with a hopeless passion for him. He is the most irresistible man in the literature of fiction." Theodora responds to Deronda as do all the unmarried female charcters in Eliot's novel. A more hostile reaction to this gender mutability appears, however, when James has the irreverent, unresponsive Pulcheria reply, "He is not a man at all!"[9]

Cross-dressing as a feature of mentorship can be traced back to the *Odyssey* as well as to the Kabbalah. In Homer's epic, the goddess Athene disguises herself as an elderly man, Mentor, in order to get Telemachus to shape up and start looking for his father. But cross-dressing in the *Odyssey* results in same-sex mentorship for Telemachus, not at all the same thing that the literary heroine finds in the nurturant male mentor. Why should her mentor, unlike that of Telemachus, be cross-sex? The requirement that a novel have a heterosexual love interest is the most obvious answer, which is why the heroine and mentor are most often romantically involved. A more speculative answer might be found in contemporary feminist psychoanalytic theory, which has drawn attention to the difficult, often painfully ambivalent relations between mother and daughter created by patriarchal socioeconomic structures. Within these structures, fantasies of rescue – to be found in numerous fairy tales, such as "Sleeping Beauty," as well as in popular romance – become associated with the father or a father figure. Judith Herman and Helen Lewis argue that the daughter meets her first disappointment when she discovers that her mother has internalized sexist codes, devaluing both herself and her daughter: "The daughter initially attempts to resolve her disappintment in her mother by turning to her father for rescue. Realizing that all the world, her mother included, sees the father as the source of freedom and power, she attempts to form a privileged relationship with her father that might exempt her from the onerous fate of an ordinary female."[10] In another revisioning of Freud's theory of penis envy, Jessica Benjamin suggests that we understand this envy in terms of the girl's experience not of the missing phallus but rather of the father. The father is "missing" for the girl in the sense that the same-sex person with whom she most closely identifies, her mother, does not in our culture figuratively represent agency, separation, autonomy, freedom, or power.[11] Represented by the father, these qualities are supposed to be appropriated by the boy, whose identificatory love for his father is, as a result, unconflicted. By contrast, the girl's identificatory love for her father is extremely problematical. Were the qualities he represents associated with the mother as well as the father, she would not be "missing" the experience of a liberating identificatory love. But since this isn't the case, a daughter is doomed to experience her identificatory love of her father as a form of betrayal, even as she imagines it to provide a way of consolidating a sense of her own agency and a means of escape.

Implicit in the psychoanalytic framework revisioned by feminists is the separation between domestic and productive spheres assumed by the novels to be considered here. Even without this framework, however, it's possible to see that the male mentor's authority derives in large part from his having – or in Deronda's case, seeking – a position in the public sphere. It's not, for example, merely differences in temperament that get Mr. Knightley associated with reason and Emma with imagination. Knightley's sound grasp of the material and social factors conditioning individual choice, demonstrated publicly when he acts as magistrate, is, implicitly, something he has gained from the experience of overseeing Donwell Abbey – experience in a much more grounded reality than that inhabited by Emma, whose imagination is fueled mainly by whim and popular fiction. *Northanger Abbey*'s Henry Tilney is a clergyman, while Edmund Bertram takes up a living by the time he and Fanny finally get together in *Mansfield Park*. *Deronda* ends with its hero embarking on a voyage to the East, having finally determined his vocation; and Lawrence Selden, Lily Bart's mentor in *Mirth*, is a lawyer, which means he has both occupation and economic independence. James's *Portrait* departs radically from this tradition, for its mentor, Touchett, not only has no occupation but is quite happy to declare himself "the idlest man living."[12] This perhaps gives him, as it gives the earlier Deronda too, a special capacity to identify with the heroine, who in all of these novels is nothing if not a woman of leisure. But unlike Deronda, Touchett retains his position as a gentleman without responsibilities; there's even a suggestion that rather than being the cause of his idleness, his invalidism merely expresses and sanctions it. Just as much as the absence of romantic interest, it's this that gives the relationship between mentor and heroine in *Portrait* its relatively undramatic, unproblematic character. For Touchett, Isabel provides a vital point of connection with the world of adventure and action upon which he looks as a spectator. This more or less reverses the situation found in *Emma*, *Deronda*, and *Mirth*, where the heroine measures herself against a standard set by her male counterpart, whose authority is legitimated by a sphere outside hers.

From the psychoanalytic perspective outlined here, the heroine's need for male mentorship comes from a desire to appropriate the freedom and power he represents. Initially, however, the heroines of *Emma*, *Deronda*, and *Mirth* don't have such a desire, being determined to escape the ordinary woman's fate entirely on their own. An awareness that might be called feminist is created in each of the novels by the clarity with which readers are asked to see the severely limited options available to the heroine. The heroines themselves, though, don't experience these limitations as opresive, and are confident of being able to impose a strongly original stamp on an as-yet-open future. Marriage, at least in its conventional, patriarchal form, is for that reason firmly resisted. All three heroines evaluate marriage solely as it relates to a prior, conventionally "masculine" determination to rule. Emma doesn't want to marry because she doesn't want to give up the position of power she enjoys as mistress of her father's house. Gwendolen plans to marry, but only because she has decided to use marriage as a means of enlarging her own exercise of power. Both she and Lily Bart violate one of the cardinal rules of both fictional and nonfictional representations of marriage in bourgeois society, which is that its real basis must be in love. The not-to-be-dwelt-upon economic foundations of the institution are assessed by Gwendolyn and Lily with clear-eyed, unabashed self-interest. Gwendolyn doesn't pretend even to herself to be in love with Grandcourt when she decides to marry him. *Deronda* makes her pay dearly for this, even while satirizing the society that encourages her attitude (the scene in which her uncle Gascoigne urges her to marry the titled, wealthy Grand-court, ignnoring the evidence of her feelings, recalls *Mansfield Park*, where Sir Bertram blithely agrees to his daughter's marriage with the rich but fatuous Rushworth). In *Mirth*, Lily's society completely supports her cooly economic viewpoint, so much so that Judith Trenor, speaking of Lily's abortive pursuit of the wealthy Percy Gryce, says to her that "we could none of us imagine your putting up with him for a moment unless you meant to marry him" (I, 7, 60).

In adopting an economic rather then sentimental view of marriage, these heroines resist an entire set of attitudes assumed to be normative for femininity. The love of rule makes exercising the power of refusal much more attractive than yielding, gracefully submitting, or assenting. It also gives the exercise of wit and ingenuity the not entirely proper pleasure of conscious superiority. The softer delights ordained for the weaker sex just won't do. When boasting to Harriet that she simply has no reason ever to marry, Emma claims that loving her nephews and nieces suits her better than a parental love that would be "warmer and blinder," and later acknowledges the absence in herself of that most winning of qualities, "tenderness of heart."[13] Tenderness of heart certainly isn't Gwendolyn's strong point, either. Having killed her sister's canary bird when its singing annoyingly vied with her own, Gwendolyn, it's safe to say, is the quintessenial *anti*sentimental heroine (tenderness for small creatures being the sine qua non of feminine sensibility). Like her double, the Alcarisi, Gwendolyn at one point actually proclaims her inability to love. She also passionately hates being made love to, as she herself declares to her mother, the only person whose bodily closeness she tolerates. This particular form of resistance seems to have been passed on, in a more subdued strain, to Lily Bart, where it is again related to a fear of losing the power of initiative. Giving it a history, Gerty Farish tells Selden, "Once, when we were children, and I had rushed up after a long separation and thrown my arms about her, she said: 'Please don't kiss me unless I ask you to, Gerty' – and she *did* ask me, a minute later; but since then I've always waited to be asked" (II, 8, 211). It's inherited even more conspiuously by Isabel Archer, who gets a heady sense of self-exaltation every time she successfully resists a suitor and who accepts Osmond only because she feels she is actively offering him something.

Portrait, however, associates this resistance with a love – empty, absurd, illusory as it is – of higher things, an ideal of independence. In this, *Portrait* his gone not to *Deronda* but rather to *Middlemarch*, whose Dorothea falls for Casaubon out of a self-deluding high-mindedness rather like Isabel's (both heroines also meet up with their disillusionment in Rome). Before she marries, Isabel's dedication to the single life has something of the purity, other-worldliness, and single-mindedness that can be found in earlier novels such as *Clarissa*, although that something is definitely viewed ironically by James. What Isabel means by "independence" would in another age have been referred to as "chastity." This, though, marks another important difference between *Portrait* and the three novels I am grouping together here. For it's not really "chastity" (originally, of course, a virtue) but rather "narcissism" that characterizes all three heroines. Indeed, one could say that it is because they are narcissistic that male mentorship is so urgently required.

Narcissism is most commonly used of the excessive love of one's own power and pleasure, excess being indicated when love of self interferes with the capacity to love or to empathize with another, which is what seems to happen in all three novels. In Freud's essay "On Narcissism" and in modern Euro-American societies generally, narcissism is a characteristic associated with women. Yet in the sheer extravagance of her delight in her own powers, the narcissist in these novels is in many ways a female rake, the rake (conventionally, of course, male) being the more developed character type on which she is patterned. The endless plotting, manipulating, and self-dramatizing in which Richardson's Lovelace, for example, takes such pleasure is exactly what Emma herself most enjoys. Like the rake, Emma enjoys upper-class privileges. She shows, as he does, an obsession with status, together with a willingness to exploit others – exactly what the action of the novel sets out to challenge. Throughout, however, Emma is free from another feature of narcissism, which is love of one's own person as an erotic object. Knightley himself says that Emma is not "personally vain," adding, "her vanity lies another way" (39). Emma's freedom from narcissism-as-vanity is part and parcel of the comic structure of Austen's novel, which liberates its heroine from her narcisstic love of power and rewards her with marriage to her mentor. By contrast, *Deronda* and *Mirth* – too modern to be swayed by the spirit of comedy – have heroines who display both kinds of narcissism. As in *Emma*, love of power is often expressed theatrically. But Gwendolyn and Lily are time and again presented in front of mirrors, as aware of the effect of their physical presence on others, and as delighting in the power communicated by their physical beauty.

It's this more sensuous narcissism, the narcissism of vanity, that in *Deronda* and *Mirth* gets bound up with the tragic shape of the action. The association of narcissism with women, simply assumed by Havelock Ellis and Freud, has more recently been placed in the context of capitalist patriarchy, with its progressive commodification of feminine attributes and concerns. Narcissism, it has been argued, is really only a pejorative term for the alienation from self experienced by women whose subjectivity has been constructed by consumer-oriented socioeconomic formations. Taking oneself as an erotic object that exists for others involves alienating one's own subjectivity, transferring it to those who behold or enjoy.[14] Contemporary feminist analyses of female narcissism aren't wildly at odds with those implicit in *Deronda* and *Mirth*. Both novels – though in *Mirth* this reaches a much more systematically supraethical level – stress the ways society itself eagerly reflects back upon the heroine the image it encourges her to flash.

To the extent that cultural pressures are made felt, the heroine's follies are seen from a perspective one might call feminist. What makes *Emma*, *Deronda*, and *Mirth* troubling, however, is that this very perspective also deprives the heroine's resistance of any radical or original content. It shows the heroine up, revealing that she's internalized the very things she imagines heroically escaping. Believing themselves to be remarkable, the heroines have desires that are, ironically, precisely those produced in women of leisure by their societies. In *Emma* this irony is communicated indirectly, as when Mrs. Elton, Emma's vulgar and inelegant double, echoes Emma's boast (which had a rather fresh, heroic ring when earlier uttered by her) about having so many independent "resources." In *Deronda* it's communicated with open relish by the narrative voice, which alternates throughout the novel between heavy satire and condescending pity ("poor Gwendolyn"). The former is what comes through in this well-known passage, which discusses the "ideal limit" – that limit being what is consistent "with the highest breeding and perfect freedom from the sordid need of income" – of Gwendolyn's "passion for doing what is remarkable":

Gwendolen was as inwardly rebellious against the restraints of family conditions as if she had been sustained by the boldest speculations; but she really had no such speculations, and would at once have marked herself off from any sort of theoretical or practically reforming women by satirising them. She rejoiced to feel herself exceptional; but her horizon was that of the genteel romance where the heroine's soul poured out in her journal is full of vague power, originality, and general rebellion, while her life moves strictly in the sphere of fashion; and if she wanders into a swamp, the pathos lies partly, so to speak, in her having on her shoes. (83)

Lily gazes out upon exactly the same horizon as does Gwendolyn. In a tone more lightly but equally satiric, Wharton describes Lily as "fond of pictures and flowers and of sentimental fiction," and as being confident "that the possession of such tastes ennobled her desire for worldly advantages" (35). With ill-masked zeal, these novels associate their heroines with the vulgarly feminine – popular romance, sentimental fiction, the journal or riddle book, a love of privilege – in order to expose the false consciousness that sustains their imaginary resistance.

Obliquely, this irony serves to establish the greatest possible distance between the idle, narcissistic heroine and her knowing, truly remarkable author. Emma draws up excellent reading lists but then spends her time with Harriet collecting riddles. Gwendolyn, too, sets herself a program of reading she can't carry through. Lily alone doesn't have such pretentions, though she clearly thinks rather more highly of the *Omar Khayyam* she carries with her than does her author. In all three novels the distance between author and heroine is further underlined, indeed thematized, by the presentation of the heroine as a kind of inauthentic artist. "Inauthentic" is perhaps too mild, though. For the heroine actively squanders her artistic talents wastefully, foolishly. Or – and the metaphor is literalized in *Mirth* – she prostitutes them. Emma, who had forsworn drawing when the portrait she made of her brother-in-law wasn't admired enough, decides to take it up again in order to do Harriet's portrait, a project undertaken for the sole purpose of forwarding her matchmaking. The narrator comments on Emma's unusual abilities and her unwillingness to "submit" to labor, concluding, "She played and sang; – and drew in almost every style; but steadiness had always been wanting; and in nothing had she approached the degree of excellence which she would have been glad to command, and ought not to have failed of" (44). In a novel that so rigorously avoids pronouncing judgement directly, this "ought" resounds with special authority. It also suggests, quietly but inevitably, a standard – moral as well as artistic – successfully met by the author of *Emma*. This very "ought" is the solemn, steadfast standard-bearer in *Emma*, *Deronda*, and *Mirth*. Its critical and – in the case of Eliot and Wharton – punitive effects subtly suggest that the unruly, artistically spendthrift heroine is a shadowy double for her disciplined, socially responsible female creator.

What does this repudiated identification mean in relation to any potentially feminist issues? Viewed historically, these novelists would seem to inherit some of the biases and conflicts of Mary Wollstonecraft's *Vindication of the Rights of Woman* (1792), the inaugural text of Euro-American feminisms. *Vindication* sets itself the task of trying to rouse its middle-class female readers from the sensual slumbers into which they have fallen, having been induced by a corrupt society to take up the vices of an idle, materialistic aristocracy. Femininity is shown to be constructed so as to make women undisciplined, self-objectifying, and so totally identified with their own overstimulated "sensibility" as to be able to live only for the moment. Women are brought up to be preoccupied with sensation, not reason, with pleasure, not duty, Wollstonecraft argues. Enthralled by throngs of particularities, they aren't able to grasp the higher, more abstract principles accessible only to a sober rationality. Since it is men who profit from this arrangement, however, women themselves shouldn't be blamed for their giddy, undignified ways. Urging an attitude at once rational and compassionate, Wollstonecraft writes, "till women are led to exercise their understandings, they should not be satirized for their attachment to rakes; or even for being rakes at heart, when it appears to be the inevitable consequence of their education. They who live to please – must find their enjoyments, their happiness in pleasure!"[15]

As Cora Kaplan has suggested, there is a kind of puritanical aggressivity in Wollstonecraft's characterizations of femininity in this text, the effect of which is to stress the workings of a debased female sexuality. At the same time, Wollstonecraft takes up a stance that can appear to be almost masculinist. For although *Vindication* asserts time and again that rationality and other virtues are intrinsically gender-neutral, it registers a conviction that, as things are, they tend to present themselves in "masculine" guise. As a result, Kaplan claims, "idealized humanity as it appears in her texts is a rational, plain speaking, bourgeois man."[16] In *Emma*, *Deronda*, and *Mirth*, the male mentor appears as the realist incarnation of this very ideal, while his wayward charge enacts the spectacle of a femininity fashioned for folly. Indeed, many of the most interesting and disturbing features of the novels examined here are given a stronger definition if they are situated in a (loosely liberal) feminist tradition originating with *Vindication*. In *Deronda* and *Mirth*, for example, the decadent, upper-class milieu functions just as the aristocracy does in *Vindication*: it highlights the connection beween leisure and a femininity constructed solely to adorn and delight. (Lest readers miss the point, *Mirth* gets Lily to dramatize it when she loses her job making high society hats – "settings for the face of fortunate womanhood" – because of her total lack of skill). Although the heroine in these novels initially resists her socialization, her vaunted independence turns out to be based on nothing solider than common feminine forms of irrationality and vice. If the heroine herself can't see this, her more enlightened mentor certainly can. His clarity of perception arises from an attitude towards self-development that is more or less the enlightened attitude proffered by *Vindication*. For this reason – in addition, of course, to his being, by virtue of his gender, a representative of the very rationality he espouses – the mentor assumes a position of special authority, for the reader as well as for the heroine.

Emma's Mr. Knightley says, early on, "There is an anxiety, a curiosity in what one feels for Emma. I wonder what will become of her!" (40) In many ways, the male mentor acts the part of what James calls the *ficelle*, the reflecting consciousness through which the main character is viewed. As *ficelle*, the mentor's anxiety and curiosity come to shape the reader's. But in the novels considered here, the mentor isn't merely a reflecting consciousness: he responds to the heroine so as actively to enlist our sympathies in the cause of refashioning her. Evidence that the mentor is a rational and plainspoken man appears whenever he engages in dialogue with the heroine. For he alone, in a society of blind admirers, refuses to flatter her. His eschewal of flattery is, of course, the other side of a high-minded belief in the possibility of the heroine's growth. In all three texts, but most insistently in *Deronda* and *Mirth*, the central conflict assumes the shape of a kind of psychomachia, a struggle in the heroine between her more debased, feminine self and her potentially virtuous self, a struggle which the mentor enters on behalf of the more genuine, though embryonic, rational or ethical self. It's the novel's action that makes this psychomachia possible, though, for only when the heroine's heroics have landed her in trouble does she have any reason to listen. Whatever its form, the heroine's resistance, shown to be imaginary, the product of false pride, has to bring about her downfall if male mentorship is to have its day. Like her more popular, less highbrow romantic sisters, the heroine has got to end up needing to be rescued – ethically or spiritually, of course – by a handsome, superior sort of man.

2

In the Anglo-American, bourgeois realist tradition, the mentor becomes, as it were, the unflattering ethical mirror in which the heroine can see a potentially rational self. By representing a different, ethically superior standard, he gets the heroine to represent her narcissistic self to a self more inward and centered. But the mirror isn't really an appropriate figure for the mentor's representational powers, nor do the novels discussed here use it. In *Deronda* and *Mirth* the mirror is linked almost exclusively to the heroine's vanity. More generally, since the seventeenth century, mirroring has been associated with women's subordinate status in the conjugal relationship, where they are to be as the moon is to the sun. In early bourgeois teachings, wives are urged to reflect in their own behavior the virtues and excellencies of their husbands. The mentor tradition basically displaces the terms of this relation, playing a nonconjugal, more woman-centered variation on a bourgeois patriarchal theme. The mentor provides a new perspective, a way of looking at things that challenges the self-complacent heroine. But this perspective ultimately can't be identified with mirrors or appearances – and not just because mirrors and men don't mix. For the mentor is to reach the heroine through her conscience, which means either through speech or by the import of his own actions. The heroine's self-dramatizing, theatrical tendencies must be checked by the still, calm voice or deeds of reason if she is to internalize the standard her male mentor sets.

The patriarchal significance of mentorship appears most clearly in Richardson's *Sir Charles Grandison*, whose hero is the novel's prototypical male mentor (if *Paradise Lost*'s Adam is disqualified). *Grandison* is important to the mentor tradition in a number of ways, besides its being Jane Austen's favorite novel. Sir Charles, the supremely virtuous central character of Richardson's novel, isn't closely imitated by any of his successors, however, partly because he plays the role of mentor to an almost endless cast of characters in this seven-volume novel. Sir Charles actively intervenes on behalf of what he judges to be the potentially virtuous future of each wayward individual he meets. Characters are lectured, cajoled, bribed, or in other ways manipulated until they are able to see that behaving as Sir Charles envisions is ultimately in their own best interests. Even when not actively shaping destinies and souls, Sir Charles is a powerful influence on those who come into contact with him, his extraordinary goodness being contagious. As one of the characters remarks, Sir Charles preaches not so much by words as by actions (VI, 667). His other-oriented, principled yet generous behavior makes everyone with whom he interacts want to become virtuous. In a novel in which the highest good is the desire to emulate goodness, Sir Charles serves as the preeminent model for nearly every character.

Idealization of Sir Charles and his effects on others is inseparable from the dominance and apparent autonomy of ethical codes in Richardson's text.[17] It is also integral to *Grandison*'s defense of patriarchy. Although this defense is multifaceted, in the following passage from a letter by Harriet Byron, the British heroine (herself, as even this short excerpt makes clear, a paragon of virtue), it takes the form of eulogizing Sir Charles's superiority over his two sisters. Reflecting on the influence Charles has on her perception of them when he returns to England, Harriet writes,

A while ago, I thought myself a poor creature, compared to these two ladies. But now I believe I am as good as they in some things. – But *they* had not such a grandmamma and aunt as I am bless'd with: *They* lost their excellent mother while they were young; and their brother is but lately come over: And his superior excellence, like sunshine, breaking out on a sudden, finds out, and brings to sight, those spots and freckles, that were hardly before discoverable. (II, 375)

What Harriet's carefully unself-righteous reflections reveal here is the valuable *critical* function performed by the idealized male mentor, who reveals imperfections in others by means of his adherence to a higher standard. *Grandison* doesn't use the term "mentor," however. "Monitor" appears instead, suggesting the specifically Protestant heritage of the male mentor's role as externalized conscience. We are often reminded that Sir Charles himself would not be the perfect gentleman he is had it not been for the influence of his own "monitor," Dr. Bartlett, who taught him at a crucial stage in his development – ever avoiding flattery – how to gain mastery over his passions. It's owing to the internalization of this "monitor" that Sir Charles can say, as the very pattern of the principled Protestant, "But I live not to the world: I live to myself; to the monitor within me" (I, 206).

For someone who doesn't live to the world, Sir Charles certainly knows a great deal about it, especially when it comes to matters that are "delicate." Women, as Sir Charles himself indicates, are supposed to be more sensitive to points of delicacy than are men. But Sir Charles, referred to by Harriet as "the most delicate-minded of men," isn't surpassed in delicacy by a single woman in the novel (VII, 425). He has, in addition, an advantage no woman does – the ability to act chivalrously. His high regard for female "honor" therefore smoothly translates into gallant behavior. To add to his attraction, delicate-mindedness, for Sir Charles, consists of a fine, almost uncanny, appreciation of the difficult, self-contradictory subject-positions available to women. What really makes Sir Charles so irresistible, though, is his active championing of female autonomy. (Three of the main female characters in Richardson's novel are madly in love with him, while, as in *Deronda*, several women can't imagine anyone else being so worthy of love). His ethical gallantry is most dramatically on display in relation to Lady Clementina, Sir Charles's Italian, Roman Catholic beloved. The principled, deeply religious Clementina is so torn between love of Sir Charles and duty (to her Deity, first, and then to her parents) that she goes mad, giving Sir Charles the very opening he needs to exercise his own high-mindedness. By contrast to her own family members, Sir Charles sacrifices his own self-interest for the sake of respecting – indeed, fostering – Lady Clementina's sense of autonomy. When Clementina's wits begin to wander, Sir Charles not only hails a British doctor but acts, himself, the part of a skilled therapist. At least in her case, mentorship is completely indistinguishable from therapy.

Harriet Byron, the British heroine Sir Charles eventually marries (once honorably freed from his commitment to the saintly Clementina) has no need at all of his mentorship. Being a virtuous woman, however, she wants to believe that she has, and so seeks his criticism. She is convinced, for example, that in a debate about learning and languages reported in letters Sir Charles later reads, she was "more lively than she ought to be, and had spoken too lightly of languages" (III, 71; VI, 249). But Sir Charles consistently declines to give her the censure she expects; Harriet's own conscience is so strong that Sir Charles delicately refuses the role of monitor. Yet if she isn't in need of spiritual guidance, the action of the novel has already challenged the unusual degree of independence she enjoys at the outset. The experience of being rescued by Sir Charles from her abductor, the lawless Sir Hargrave, creates in Harriet new feelings of vulnerability. Strong gratitude turns into love of her protector. But love of such a man as Sir Charles in turn gives way to the newfound sense of unworthiness and secondariness her entrance into marriage demands. As a result of this humbling, Harriet becomes the blushing, tremulous maid she is supposed to be if she is to marry Sir Charles. Instead of correcting, Sir Charles then has to strengthen her, as he does, for example, at their public wedding ceremony, when he exhorts the failing Harriet at least to appear happy in order to honor the choice she has made.

So virtuous is Sir Charles that even his being in love with two women is admirable. He loves each woman for her transcendent goodness, magnanimously declaring Harriet and Clementina to be "Sister-excellencies" (VII, 343). Idealization of Sir Charles (who obviously *has* to be delicate to handle this situation) is married to an idealization of relations between the two women, neither of whom experiences the sordid emotion of jealousy. Earlier on, Harriet finds herself worrying that love might be "a narrower of the heart" (II, 387). But since the novel demands exemplary behavior, Harriet's heart grows to encompass an ardent admiration of both Sir Charles and Clementina, who becomes "My next-to Divine Monitress" (VI, 165). Although *Grandison* upholds monogamy, Sir Charles's spiritual polygamy is clearly tolerated, as is the sexual double standard on which it rests. Sir Charles himself acknowledges that he wouldn't have been very happy with a love "double" or "divided" the way his own is. His liberal, unconventionally broadminded notions are also shown when he becomes an advocate of his late father's mistress, whom he treats with generosity and respect. Rationally weighing the particulars of Mrs. Oldham's character – her touching humility, her orderliness and ability to manage – and her situation – the existence of children, his father's honor – Sir Charles judges on sound patriarchal grounds that she is worthy of protection and support. This might be a delicate matter, but we are left in no doubt as to *Grandison*'s stand on the issue. Though his two sisters respond to Mrs. Oldham with hostility and a desire to shame her, the virtuous Harriet entirely shares Sir Charles's views. Indeed, her eulogy of their brother, quoted earlier, is delivered after he has reprimanded his sisters for their small-mindedness. The headstrong Charlotte later reveals that they have been properly humbled by Sir Charles when she says to the now-betrothed Harriet, "Remember, you have a man to deal with, who, from our behaviour to Mrs. Oldham, at his first return to England, took measure of our minds, and, without loving us the less for it, looked down upon us with pity; and made us, ever since, look upon ourselves in a diminishing light, and as sisters who have greater reason to glory in their brother, than he has in them" (VI, 68).

3

Austen's Mr. Knightley, the most well-known descendent of Sir Charles, inherits this particular mantle in concerning himself throughout *Emma* with the heroine's treatment of other women. He lectures Emma on the inequality between herself and her pro-tegée Harriet, who behaves toward Emma like the ideally sub-missive wife (taking up Mrs. Weston's role). And he urges her to become a friend of Jane Fairfax, too accomplished and reserved to be the object of Emma's attentions. The climax of the novel occurs at the Box Hill outing, when Mr. Knightley takes Emma to task for her taunting of Miss Bates. In *The Writing of Fiction*, when Wharton illustates effective fiction's use of what she calls the "illuminating incident," it's this scene from *Emma* that she chooses – "Emma losing her temper with Miss Bates at the picnic."[18] Because Miss Bates is relatively poor as well as single, in attacking her Emma betrays not only her sex. Emma's earlier pronouncements on the advantages to her of remaining single weren't graced by any altruistic notions, as is conventional in such a defense. (When Grandison's Harriet, for example, deliv-ers a defense of the single life, she gives further proof of a virtu-ous solidarity with her sex [II, 232].) They were also classist, and specifically with reference to Miss Bates. Emma has already vio-lated the bond of sisterhood (with regard to both Harriet and Jane). But her high-spirited put-down of Miss Bates puts the fin-ishing touches to her portrait as a heartless heroine. Recalling Emma to a sense of her class-based responsibility to protect her inferiors, Knightley says, "Her situation should secure your com-passion" – "secure" being the appropriate word here, not "move" (375).

Knightley intervenes with a speech in which the moral and social meaning of Emma's behavior towards Miss Bates is put to her, represented. That this is a crisis becomes clear when for the first time Emma doesn't in any way resist her mentor. We are told she feels the full force of Knightley's words: "Never had she felt so agitated, mortified, grieved, at any circumstance in her life. She was most forcibly struck. The truth of his represen-tation there was no denying. She felt it at her heart" (376).

"Representation" here (as on other occasions in Austen and Richardson) has a slightly negative, vaguely legalistic connotation, as if Emma feels herself having been brought by Knightley's charges to the bar of justice. Knightley's moral authority is consistently associated with his strong purchase on reality, presented as infinitely greater than Emma's. Implicitly, therefore, Emma develops an analogy between the mentor's morally motivated "representation" and the very representational mode of Austen's realist text – an analogy that is more insistently if less sublty drawn in *Northanger Abbey*. When Emma accepts the truth of Knightley's representation, submitting not only to his mentorship but to reality itself, the novel's comic impulses can take over, structuring her response in the form of a conversion to the good. The haughty, willful Emma breaks down weeping, a sign of inward repentance that is followed by tangible evidence of psychological change, such as her persisting in overtures to Jane Fairfax in spite of rebuffs.

Most of Emma's errors of interpretation are connected, though much less obviously than in *Northanger Abbey*, to a consumption of too-light fiction, or at least to an uncritical imbibing of popular female culture. Emma's conviction that Harriet Smith is the daughter of a noble father, for example, is clearly the product of her reading (Harriet, it turns out, isn't Evelina; the demythologizing Knightley doubts that Harriet has any "respectable relations," and, once sobered up, Emma confronts the ugly, unadorned "stain of illegitimacy, unbleached by nobility or wealth" [61, 482]). The intrigue Emma concocts for Jane Fairfax involves the unsuspecting Mr. and Mrs. Dixon in a clandestine romantic triangle. In this case, Austen gives us an instance of what we now call projection (again, more obviously at work in *Northanger Abbey*), since Emma herself has the rivalrous feelings she attributes to Jane Fairfax and is structurally a romantic rival in a way that even the reader can't know at this stage in the novel. In her conversation with Miss Bates, the detail that really fires Emma's overheated imagination is that Mr. Dixon once rendered Jane Fairfax a service – interpreted by Emma to mean "he saved her life" – in an accident at sea (217). That any act of gallantry or rescue should necessarily either bring about or signify romantic passion is the most important assumption inspiring Emma's imaginings. In the very first chapter, she claims to have "planned" the match between Miss Taylor and Mr. Weston from the moment "when, because it began to mizzle, he darted away with so much gallantry, and borrowed two umbrellas for us from farmer Mitchell's" (12). When later on she finds Harriet has been rescued from gypsies by Frank Churchill, Emma immediately concludes that a spark has been ignited between them that will almost certainly result in marriage, while the narrator sends her up, merrily, as an "imaginist" (335).

Emma deliberately involves the reader in the highly inventive, vigorous mental process whereby Emma gets odd scraps of evidence to fit her ingenious, romance-rooted ideas. Wollstonecraft's *Vindication* tries to account for fanciful cerebral activity like Emma's, arguing that because women are "restrained from entering into more important concerns by political and civil oppression, sentiments become events, and reflection deepens what it should, and would have effaced, if the understanding had been allowed to take a wider range" (306). But if this is to apply to Emma, the "sentiments" that "become events" should be changed to "ideas about sentiments," for in each and every instance Emma deduces what others must be feeling from her own sentimental ideas about their destinies. Emma has, in spades, the "romantic twist of mind" Wollstonecrafts sees inculcated in women, who often get so absorbed in reflections on "love" that "in the midst of these sublime refinements they plump into actual vice" (305, 6). Knightley indicates, early on, that Emma's matchmaking is decidedly improper. Unlike Sir Charles, who is able to act as stage director with impunity, Emma's manipulation of others proceeds not from prudent fidelity to the good but haphazardly, first from "sublime refinements," and second from class-based pride (as in Emma's conviction that Robert Martin isn't good enough for an intimate friend of hers).

By contrast to the true mentor, Emma uses mentorship as an occasion for self-display. Together with her skill in the arts of concealment, her self-dramatizing tendencies are, early on, a sure sign she's not a proper bourgeois heroine, for whom hatred of anything smacking of theatricality is de rigeur. As I've already suggested, Emma's snobbishness, quick wit, and persistence in plots of her own devising establish her kinship with the male rake. But by far the most important characteristic she shares with him is her inability to empathize with others. Traditionally, the rake plays with his victim's feelings by raising expectations he will not fulfill. That he does this because he is morally or psychologically deficient is always made abundantly clear. In *Sense and Sensibility*, it is said of Willoughby that "he had already done that, which no man who *can* feel for another, would do" (209). Willoughby has also done what only a *man* could do, for he has seduced, abandoned, and thereby ruined the now-pregnant Eliza. But a similar inability to feel for another informs Emma's actions, as it does Frank Churchill's. That Emma's fellow flirt Frank turns out to be safely this side of actual rakehood shows that *Emma* consistently makes use of a domesticated version of the rake. But in Emma's matchmaking Austen has devised the perfect vehicle for her heroine's figurative libertinism. Time and again Emma leads Harriet to expect a declaration, a proposal of marriage, while positioning herself outside the charmed circle of romance. For the sake of gratifying her own pleasure, Emma takes possession of Harriet, getting her to sacrifice her would-be husband, Robert Martin, together with his family. Ever on her own guard, the tireless Emma is, finally, quite as ready to jeopardize her pretty friend's future as any libertine his similarly unprotected, socially inferior beloved.

Emma's manifold ironies measure its distance from the idealizing mode of *Grandison*, which has the romantic attachment of its mentor-hero and heroine originate in a dramatic scene of solidly physical rescue: Sir Charles bravely delivers Harriet from her libertine captor. The chivalrous Sir Charles frequently seems to utter sentiments one might call feminist. But when participating in a debate on the relations of the sexes, he reveals his true colors by becoming an advocate of male supremacy. In part because it would be rather indelicate to lay too much stress on male intellectual superiority, Sir Charles turns the ability to rescue into the cornerstone of patriarchal relations:

I, for my part, would only contend, that we men should have power and right given us to protect and serve your Sex; that we purchase and build for them; travel and toil for them; run through, at the call of Providence, or of our King and Country, dangers and difficulties; and, at last, lay our trophies, all our acquirements, at your feet; enough rewarded in the conscience of duty done, and your favourable acceptance. (VI, 248, 49)

In the phrase "should have power and right given us" there is an interesting gesture toward the notion of contract. Power and right aren't assumed on the grounds of superior strength but are instead to be granted by women. Carole Pateman has shown how the marriage "contract" implicitly offers women protection in return for the obedience that is explicitly vowed. Since women aren't fully party to either the social or the sexual contract, the fiction of consent or acceptance has to be carefully protected.[19] *Grandison* does this, at the same time that it wisely stresses not the servitude implied by obedience but the devoted service provided by the dutiful protector. By means of Sir Charles's rhetorical sleight of hand, women (first "they" and then an idealized "you") seem to be able to command the very service men can then claim they have the "right" to bestow – a "right" implicitly symbolic of patriarchal privilege itself.

Although Sir Charles's female auditors are completely won over by his defense, Jane Austen, Richardson's admirer, may not have been so readily persuaded.[20] In its systematic send-up of romantic readings of gallantry and rescue, *Emma* seems to enact a spirited resistance to Richardson's seductive idealization of patriarchal relations. (Even Mr. Knightley's knightliness is revisioned: "He is not a gallant man, but he is a very humane one," Emma asserts [222].) In any event, rescue is in Austen's works thoroughly transposed to the ethico-psychological plane. If it's effected at all, it's not by deeds of heroic daring but rather by the mentor's example and words. Even this formulation is a bit too crude, however, for "rescue" of any sort deflects attention away from the kind of subjective process required by Austen's realism. She who is in need of rescue must anyway go her own way. This is why toward the end of the novel Knightley depreciates his mentorship, claiming he could easily have harmed Emma by his interference. This is also why *Emma* represents the process of change by means of two distinct climaxes, of which Emma is clearly the subject. The first, which has already been discussed, is categorically moral: Emma's mortified response to Knightley's harangue at the Box Will outing. In addition to newly contrite behavior, Emma's conversion to the good takes the form of a new appreciation (born out of disappointment with Frank Churchill) of "that upright integrity, that strict adherence to truth and principle, that disdain of trick and littleness, which a man should display in every transaction of his life" (397). While leading, unconsciously, to the love of Knightley she will soon experience, Emma's embracing of this new standard reveals how love of her male mentor is already giving her – as is proper in a patriarchal society – a new ideal for herself.[21]

Knightley isn't an agent of change in the second climax, however, in which passion acts as the catalyst of a shift in self-awareness. In a moment of almost classic *anagnorisis* – which, ideally, coincides with the *peripeteia*, the protagonists's change of fortune – Emma abruptly discovers her true feelings about Knightley when Harriet reveals that she is in love with him. As in the earlier scene, there's an emphasis on the "truth" and on her "heart," which she nows struggles to understand. Yet this revelation is paired with another, equally important, into the folly of her matchmaking:

Her own conduct, as well as her own heart, was before her in the same few minutes. She saw it all with a clearness which had never blessed her before. How improperly had she been acting by Harriet! How inconsiderate, how indelicate, how irrational, how unfeeling had been her conduct! What blindness, what madness, had led her on! It struck her with dreadful force, and she was ready to give it every bad name in the world. (408)

Austen represents Emma's two revelations – of her love and of her folly – as occuring simultaneously. This is because the moment Emma experiences being truly in love is at the very same time the moment she ceases to be a kind of rake, for whom the feelings of others have little or no reality. That the capacity to love another is linked to the capacity to empathize is an insight that also appears in *Sensibility*, in the scene where Willoughby owns his heartless treatment of Marianne to her sister Elinor. Acknowledging that he had callously sought "to engage her regard without a thought of returning it," he defends himself, feelingly, "But one thing may be said for me, even in that horrid state of selfish vanity, I did not know the extent of the injury I meditated, because I did not *then* know what it was to love" (320). Whether Wllloughby has indeed ever truly loved another is a question *Sensibility* leaves open. He is, after all, a real rake, and although Austen seems committed to considering the possibility that rakes might reform, she doesn't ever actually represent it. Emma, however, never a full-fledged rake, undergoes what is supposed to amount to a complete conversion.

But here, too, Austen refuses the idealizing mode of *Grandison*. Although *Emma* fully acknowledges the harm she has done Harriet, she is not able to transcend the rivalry that has now entered their relations. If Harriet gets what Emma wants, Emma will, of course, behave properly, with justice; but that doesn't mean pretending she won't be distressed and forever miserable. Austen doesn't intend to put her through this ordeal, of course, and Knightley soon proposes to Emma, at which point the novel's overthrow of idealized relations between women becomes almost aggressively doctrinaire:

[F]or as to any of that heroism of sentiment which might have prompted her to entreat him to transfer his affection from herself to Harriet, as infinitely the most worthy of the two – or even the more simple sublimity of resolving to refuse him at once and for ever, without vouchsafing any motive, because he could not marry them both, Emma had it not. She felt for Harriet, with pain and with contrition; but no flight of generosity run mad, opposing all that could be probable or reasonable, entered her brain. She had led her friend astray, and it would be a reproach to her for ever; but her judgment was as strong as her feelings, and as strong as it had ever been before, in reprobating any such alliance for him, as most unequal and degrading. (431)

Liberated from the shackles of feminine fancy, Emma's mind now works with Knightley-like ease and clarity within the fixed, hierarchical structures of her time. Realism, here, takes the form of an unillusioned acceptance of class stratification. More chillingly, it involves the calm and assured acceptance of class-privileged entitlement. Emma knows what is her due and is unconflicted about wanting it, even though it might come at the cost of someone else's pain. Happily, the novel's comic closure returns Harriet to her proper mate, Robert Martin. But there is a brief moment, here, when the the newly reformed heroine gets permission to be just as willing to sacrifice the illegitimate Harriet as was her repudiated double, the female (figurative) rake.

4

In spite of obvious and enormous differences, *Emma* (which Eliot read aloud with Lewes) is an important influence on *Daniel Deronda*.[22] To begin with, in addition to the general resemblances sketched above, *Deronda*'s heroine is, like *Emma*'s, "spoiled." Although this is implicit in *Emma*'s opening lines, Knightley uses the adjective three times, and Book I of *Deronda*, which introduces us to Gwendolyn, goes even further, being entitled "The Spoiled Child." Both novels indicate that the heroine's love and exercise of power is in part the result of her having been (to use a current term) "parentified." Emma, taking the place of her late mother, parents her elderly father, while Gwendolyn, in a more unusual substitution, assumes her late father's place as her mother's husband. Class privilege (in Gwendolyn's case, like Lily's, insecurely held) serves to reinforce the sense of exceptional powers. But even more significant as a point of similarity is the emphasis both novels place on the heroine's exploitative use of art. In both, this is underlined by the presence of secondary characters whose attitudes and skills meet with more approval than the heroine's. While there are several such characters in *Deronda*, *Emma*'s Jane Fairfax has her exact counterpart in *Deronda*'s Catherine Arrowpoint. Both are presented as disciplined and accomplished pianists, who are relatively unassuming and even *too* reserved. Yet they, not the heroines, have passionate and transgressively romantic relationships. When the Arrowpoints threaten to disown their daughter if she marries Klesmer, Catherine shows that she has, besides, the "bold speculations" *Deronda*'s heroine lacks.

Gwendolyn, like Emma, fails to feel the "emulative Love" *Grandison* expects from its virtuous women when meeting up with superior souls. Richardson's novel deeply impressed Eliot when she first read it, and in many ways *Grandison* is even more important to *Deronda* than it is to *Emma*.[23] Although the term "mentor" appears as early as Chapter 2, one minor sign of possible influence is the use, elsewhere, of "monitor" (with reference to both Klesmer and Grandcourt). Much more important is the fact that in both novels the hero – whose name serves as the title – stars in the role of mentor, the upright Deronda, like Sir Charles, being capable of every "delicacy of feeling" (207). The structuring of the hero's relations provides the most crucial sign of intertextuality, however. In both novels the hero is involved with two women, each of whom is a heroine in her own right. What makes this acceptable – in addition, of course, to the hero's great virtue, which obscures the role of the sexual double standard – is that the two women come from different, indeed opposing, cultures. More precisely – and this draws the two novels uncannily close – in both *Grandison* and *Deronda* one of the heroines is English while the other is "foreign," with religious beliefs not tolerated by England's Protestantism. Moreover, in both, the hero meets the English heroine after his affections have already been engaged by her foreign rival. *Deronda*'s opening in medias res, frequently discussed, displaces the chronological beginning just as does *Grandison*'s, and to the same effect: the reader is kept in the dark about the existence of the foreign rival, being led, instead, to think the English heroine to be the sole object of the hero's attentions.

The English heroine, Harriet Byron, ultimately triumphs in the comic *Grandison*. In turning to Harriet, Sir Charles returns – family and friends rejoicing – to his God as to his country, which in time he plans to serve in public office. By contrast with the male members of Clementina's family, who are bigoted, rigid, and ruthless in pursuing their ends, Sir Charles is a model of right-minded liberality. In the most difficult of circumstances, he upholds both his Protestantism and his patriotism in a dignified, gentlemanly fashion. Richardson draws on a variety of popular, well-established nationalist (and specifically anti-Italian) traditions to articulate his vision of a supremely civilized, Protestant England. Eliot, however, reaches outside these very traditions to mount a critique of the racism and parochialism of the upper-class English society of her day. Like Austen, Eliot resists the idealizations of *Grandison*, but on a grander, more overtly political scale. As a result, the conflicted *Deronda* almost systematically overturns the more complacent resolutions of *Grandison*. Far from affirming his Englishness, Deronda's hero comes to reject it altogether, deciding to leave England for the East when he discovers that he is Jewish. Where Sir Charles finally marries the thoroughly English Harriet, Deronda ends up marrying the Jewish Mirah, who is a figure of pathos in much the way Clementina is. It is Gwendolyn, though, whose situation really resembles Clementina's. Both Sir Charles and Deronda marry women who haven't required their mentorship, while the needy Gwendolyn and Clementina are left to face life without their beloved mentors. With regard to *Deronda*'s hero, the English Gwendolyn therefore ends up not in the position of the happy bride but of the distressed, Italian Clementina: she is the outsider, the Dido who won't be able to share with Aeneas his forging of a nation. Through the eyes of admiring sisters, the married Gwendolyn is once compared to the beautiful Harriet Byron, heroine of Richardson's nationalist epic, in what must be *Deronda*'s most ironic allusion.

The romantic Clementina's "malady" can be discussed in terms of a "raised imagination." As several critics have emphasized, Gwendolyn's malady, much more modern, is interestingly pathologized, almost seeming to invite psychoanalytic labels such as "narcissistic," "hysterical," "agoraphobic." Using the less medicalized terms of current popular psychology, Gwendolyn can be seen to be "split" between a false self, which is highly controlled, commanding, and articulate, and a hidden self able to express itself only in silence, screams, and tears. From this perspective, the unspecified dread haunting Gwendolyn is the dread of releasing the powerful emotions associated with this hidden, undeveloped self. No matter what the interpretative framework, though, attention given to Gwendolyn's troubled psychic states makes Deronda's mentorship a very different thing from Knightley's.[24]

Although the narrator tells us that Gwendolyn turns Deronda into a "priest," it's obvious now that he is feeling his way into the therapist's role (485). The process whereby Emma comes to idealize Knightley is one of ethical growth but also of romantic involvement ending in marriage. In *Deronda*, the relationship between mentor and heroine is, at best, only ambiguously romantic, with the result that Gwendolyn's idealization of Deronda comes to have the curiously subjective, suspended quality of psychotherapeutic transference. The novel's discourse longs to turn ethical concerns into spiritual ones. But in its leisured, upper-class English setting, the heightened, paratheological language used to describe Gwendolyn's "conversion" slides back, willy-nilly, into the space it opens up for a thoroughly secular intersubjectivity.

This displacement of the romantic dimension of the mentor-heroine relationship is related to the awkwardly bifurcated, bi-formal character of *Deronda*. Romance motifs and structure seem to have legitimacy only in the Jewish realm, where quests are completed, true parentage discovered, reunions celebrated, and destinies fulfilled. Deronda's relationship with Mirah originates in a classically romantic action: Deronda saves Mirah from death by drowning. As with Sir Charles and Harriet, the scene of rescue awakens feeling and attachment on both sides. It also confers on the male rescuer the right to continue offering protection and support. When Daniel enters Gwendolyn's world, it is to attempt a spiritual rescue of this English maiden-in-distress. He ends up contrasting the two forms of rescue, however, recognizing that Gwendolyn "too needed a rescue, and one much more difficult than that of the wanderer by the river – a rescue for which he felt himself helpless" (620). When, in Genoa, Gwendolyn herself needs to be rescued from death by drowning, it's an unknown fisherman who comes to her aid, not Deronda. Rescue by her mentor isn't afforded Gwendolyn, and not only because, like Emma, she must come to a new self on her own. By permitting romance only elsewhere, in Deronda's world, *Deronda* asks us to see Gwendolyn as mired, inescapably, in the real, having been constructed once and for all by the social and material forces the novel painstakingly details.

For Gwendolyn, then, there is no quest but rather pursuit – pursuit of her as an object of desire (Rex and Grandcourt) or of revenge (Mrs. Glasher and the Furies). There is flight instead of rescue, abandonment in the place of reunion, and fulfillment only of what she dreads. When Gwendolyn leaps into the water, she not only doesn't save Grandcourt from death by drowning but doesn't unambiguously even attempt to do so, simultaneously enacting her worst fears. Gwendolyn longs to be rescued by Deronda. But almost as often as he feels the desire to rescue her it is thwarted, for the strength of Gwendolyn's own self-absorption acts as a rebuff: "It was as if he saw her drowning while his limbs were bound" (509). This self-preoccupation comes in part, though, from Gwendolyn's own intense fear of abandonment. When confronting a life without Sir Charles, the lovelorn Clementina at least has the consolation of knowing she has consciously renounced him. But Gwendolyn begs Deronda over and over again not to leave her – as he finally does.

In the scenes in which Gwendolyn and Deronda speak to one another, time, which is always stolen time, becomes suspended, together with the conventions of ordinary social interaction. Much is communicated nonverbally, but what isn't said in these dialogues – in contrast to those in which she vies for power with Grandcourt – conveys the sense of Gwendolyn's transparent vulnerability. A childlike self emerges, frightened but demanding, while struggling for integration with her adult self's now shattered sense of agency. Since only Deronda (and the reader) witness this self, otherwise disguised by the self-consciously dramatic efforts of Gwendolyn to "represent" her successful marriage, it takes on the status of the authentic self, capable of establishing its own creative bonds. Yet the peculiar intimacy that results from this regression produces an atmosphere of illicitness in these scenes. From the feminist psychoanalytic perspective sketched earlier, the intensely idealizing love the childlike Gwendolyn feels for her male mentor resembles the girl's identificatory love of the father. As was mentioned, in a patriarchal society this love will tend to feel illigitimate, since it involves betraying the mother, not perceived as a full subject or agent. On a strictly narrative level, it's of course Gwendolyn's marriage that produces the effect of illicitness, for the closeness of her relations with Deronda stirs up something very like jealousy in her husband, who always threatens to interrupt their meetings. Although Gwendolyn is certainly aware of the interpretation that might be given her relationship with Deronda, she is presented as being completely without the desire that would make it actually adulterous. Like Clementina, she doesn't feel what she isn't supposed to be feeling. In spite of good intentions, however, romantic interest hovers in the wings of every transgressive encounter. The coarseness of the worldly Sir Hugo's remarks should make us want to dismiss any suggestion of impropriety from our minds. But Deronda himself is able to do so only with persistent, conscious effort, and until the very end regards Gwendolyn as an attractive object of potential – or, on account of Mirah, sort of hypothetical – romantic interest.

These encounters, which provide a pattern for Wharton's *Mirth*, are themselves perhaps influenced by a scene in Austen's *Sensibility* in which Willoughby, now a repentant rake, reveals his feelings to Elinor, the sister of the woman he has jilted, Marianne. A sense of impropriety intermittently haunts this scene, since, like Gwendolyn, Willoughby is now married and has no business, as Elinor is aware, pouring out his love for Marianne. As in *Deronda*, it seems to be the very absence of romantic involvement between the interlocutors that makes possible such frank discussion. Yet the risk of impropriety seems to attach itself to interaction with the rake. In Austen's novel, Willoughby verbally seduces Elinor, woman of sense, who is brought by him to experience a compassion she rationally resists and later disowns. Like Gwendolyn, the spoiled Willoughby has married for money, not love, thereby proving himself to be hopelessly impulsive and selfish. Now that he's miserable, however, Willoughby urgently wants to explain himself, which he proceeds to do at great length, Elinor vacillating throughout the exchange between hardening her heart against him and a softening, a sympathy she cannot, in spite of herself, withhold. Although the properly schooled reader of Austen remains skeptical, Willoughby's professions of sincere remorse and continuing, painful attachment move the susceptible Elinor, temporarily suspending her otherwise sharp moral sense.

Their conversation ends with Willoughby asking for reassurance and even a kind of commitment:

"And you *do* think something better of me than you did?" – said he . . . leaning against the mantel-piece as if forgetting he was to go.

Elinor assured him that she did; – that she forgave, pitied, wished him well – was even interested in his happiness – and added some gentle counsel as to the behaviour most likely to promote it. His answer was not very encouraging.

"As to that," said he, "I must rub through the world as well as I can. Domestic happiness is out of the question. If, however, I am allowed to think that you and yours feel an interest in my fate and actions, it may be the means – it may put me on my guard – at least, it will be something to live for. Marianne to be sure is lost to me forever. Were I even by any blessed chance at liberty again" –

Elinor stopped him with a reproof. (331, 32)

Gwendolyn enters her marriage with a conscience even more troubled than Willoughby's, having broken her promise to Lydia Clasher. But Eliot's novel wants to put the sincerity of Gwendolyn's remorse beyond question when time and again she turns to Deronda with the very same broken, halting speech and beseeching tones. Gender plays a major role in distinguishing the two rakes, for where Willoughby can seem to be manipulative (even if unconsciously so), Gwendolyn becomes tremulously childlike when expressing repentance. Together with the absence of adulterous desire (the presence of which, in Willoughby, triggers Elinor's reproof), this transparency ensures that Gwendolyn's mentor isn't in any danger of being seduced, Gwendolyn being, implicitly, thoroughly deserving of the unconditional support he provides.

For Gwendolyn, as for Willoughby, domestic happiness is out of the question. But where Willoughby drops out of *Sensibility* after his conversation with Elinor, Gwendolyn continues to hold center stage after entering her disastrous marriage. *Deronda* is thereby able to develop *Sensibility*'s connecting of moral improvement with the ability to be on one's guard. Specifically,

Willoughby's veiled threat, in the scene just quoted, seems to inform the struggling-to-be-penitent Gwendolyn's many appeals to Deronda; paraphrased, the appeal/threat goes something like: "only if you truly care about me do I have any chance of living up to your standards, or of having the strength to be on guard against my own tendencies." Gwendolyn, however, has the demonic force of her hatred of Grandcourt to contend with. *Deronda* therefore gets her mentor to deliver these monitory words, which repeat themselves within her as a kind of charm: "Turn your fear into a safeguard. Keep your dread fixed on the idea of increasing that remorse which is so bitter to you" (509). To ensure her receptivity, *Deronda* has Gwendolyn experience not just the rake's occasional fit of remorse but the torments of the damned. Only turbulent, murderous (self-)hatred, it seems, is strong enough to turn Gwendolyn's unspecific dread into a force of resistance to her own destructive impulses.

Resistance of this sort, though, is really a form of submission, and one recommended by Deronda: submission to the influence of one's mentor and his belief in an as-yet-unrealized self. "Resistance" and its cognates appear with great frequency in *Deronda*, but its value is determined by a double standard. At times resistance is lauded as a healthy, progressive form of protest, as when Gwendolyn actively resists the poisonous influence of Grandcourt's cynicism. Her bondage to Grandcourt becomes unbearably painful when even her resistance is, finally, successfully cowed: "To resist was to act like a stupid animal unable to measure results" (745). Mordecai cries out, "Woe to the men who see no place for resistance in this generation!" and goes on to say that in a time of spiritual inaction, the prophet or leader will be he whose "very soul is resistance, and is as a seed of fire that may enkindle the souls of multitudes, and make a new pathway for events" (585, 86). Earlier in the novel, however, resistance, associated with Gwendolyn, is viewed more critically as a willful and defensive reflex. "Resistance" appears in the first two chapters in connection with the defiant rage that keeps Gwendolyn gambling after Deronda's gaze has jinxed her as well as with the anger that possesses her when she has to face her loss (39, 45). References to Gwendolyn's "resistant temper," her "haughty resistant speeches," her "resistant self," or "the unpleasant tone of resistance with which she had met his recommendation of Mirah" all point to the unruly, combative force of Gwendolyn's narcissitic or false self, the self that in *Deronda* has to be brought low (177, 276, 356, 493).

So, it would seem, must be the strong, rebellious self of the Alcarisi, *Deronda*'s other unruly woman, who resists her father's wishes and rejects her maternal role in order to become a successful artist. When Deronda meets up with the woman who abandoned him as a child, she reveals that the past she repudiated has come now to take its revenge:

"It was my nature to resist, and say, 'I have a right to resist'. Well, I say so still when I have any strength in me. You have heard me say it, and I don't withdraw it. But when my strength goes, some other right forces itself upon me like iron in an inexorable hand; and even when I am at ease, it is beginning to make ghosts upon the daylight. And now you have made it worse for me." (699)

Although Deronda makes it worse, the process of Alcarisi's bitter conversion begins when she falls under the influence of a forceful monitor. Joseph Kalonymos, her father's representative, puts to her in words the shameful horror of her deeds, at which point her conscience is bitten: "This man's words were like lion's teeth upon me. My father's threats eat into me with my pain" (702). In relation to Gwendolyn, it's Mrs. Glasher's words that have this terrifying effect, Deronda's role being less violent, less exclusively punitive. Yet on one occasion, when Gwendolyn tells Deronda about her part in her husband's drowning, she recalls Deronda's monitory words in language as visceral as Alcarm's: "It was all like a writing of fire within me" (760).

As Gwendolyn's mentor, Deronda assists in awakening her conscience so it can monitor her rebellious impulses. The dominance in *Deronda* of monitory, judgmental attitudes results, however, in a strangely decentred narrative of the heroine's development. Deronda, emergent patriarch, finds continuities, sequence, and the hope of an organic center, while Gwendolyn struggles hopelessly, endlessly, to transform a resistant self. By contrast with Emma, there is no dramatic *anagnorisis* for Gwendolyn but instead a series of partial awakenings that seem always to leave her basically unchanged. Where Emma develops the capacity for empathy through an experience of love, Gwendolyn is introduced to it by applying to herself Deronda's harsh words about not making one's gain someone else's loss. We're meant to see this as an important moment in "an uneasy, transforming process" likened to conversion (477). But the process goes on and on, being both intensified and frustrated by Grandcourt's abuse. Typically, a conversion narrative moves from a state of proud self-complacency on the part of its subject through a crisis of doubt and self-alienation to a final state of newly consolidated spiritual strength. Although the chastened, stricken Gwendolyn can say to Deronda, "But if I go on, I shall get worse. I want not to get worse. I should like to be what you wish," she does, anyway, go on, and she doesn't ever become what Deronda wishes (672). Gwendolyn receives several lectures from Deronda on the importance of developing a disinterested love of higher things. But either she hasn't grasped a thing he's said or the narrative doesn't want to credit her with it, for when Deronda reveals his destiny to Gwendolyn, we're told that she was "for the *first* time being dislodged from her supremacy in her own world" (my italics) (876). As this antidevelopmental ordering suggests, *Deronda* places its heroine in a state of almost perpetual crisis. When at the end of the novel her mentor forsakes her, Gwendolyn is left with only her determination to "resist self-despair" (867).

Befitting its bi-formal character, there are two kinds of fulfillment in *Deronda*, both based on a kind of "second-sight."[25] Mordecai's desire for the continuation of his own spiritual self in Deronda is fully satisfied, and the language of typology is used to characterize the relationship between his imaged wish and its fulfillment. For Gwendolyn, however, there is only the realization of what is feared, for which neither theology nor psychoanalysis has a name. When Gwendolyn responds hysterically to Grandcourt's drowning, convinced that she has murdered him, it's because his death comes as a fulfillment of her murderous desires: "I only know that I saw my wish outside me" (761). Yet the scene of Grandcourt's drowning also refers back to the scene depicted on the panel, which so inexplicably terrified

Gwendolyn: in both appear an upturned face as well as a fleeing figure. When Grandcourt drowns, Gwendolyn's consciousness is flooded by the strength of her own murderous impulses, making her feel that she actually fled from him, abandoning him as he drowned. Earlier, this picture makes a dramatic, Gothic appearance at the very moment Gwendolyn is to enact Hermione's transition from statue-as-death to life in a *tableau* representing the scene of miraculous awakening in *The Winter's Tale*. Gwendolyn's dread-filled, hysterical response to the picture makes it impossible for her to play her part, figuratively suggesting an incapacity for self-transformation. In addition to embodying the figures in the panel, the scene of her husband's death by drowning reenacts her paralysis in this abortive *tableau*. For in this later scene, too, Gwendolyn fails to act a part – namely, the part of her mentor's reforming, perfectible rake.

Ever the faithful mentor, Deronda believes implicitly in Gwendolyn's innocence even before hearing her story. And Gwendolyn assures him over and over again that the memory of his words was her only safeguard. But more closely examined, Deronda's influence seems severely limited – limited, specifically, to inspiring Gwendolyn's throwing herself into the water *after* she is sure her hateful husband has drowned. According to her account – which is, significantly, all we have – her internal conflict virtually paralyzes her so long as Grandcourt calls for help. It's only when he goes down for the third time that Daniel's words really take hold, for then, the death a reality, she knows that she doesn't want to have to live with the image of herself as a "murderess." When she first tries to talk, Gwendolyn tells Deronda that his words "came to me at the very last – that was the reason why I – "(755). Were Gwendolyn's speech not quite so broken it would perhaps be more obvious that she jumps not to save her husband's life but instead to rescue her better self from the harsh, exacting conscience Deronda is now a part of. By leaping in when it's too late to save Grandcourt, Gwendolyn willingly risks her life in a desperate, last-ditch attempt to protect the image of the potentially good self Deronda has fostered.

Deronda itself isn't at all sure it wants to protect Gwendolyn, however. (In part, perhaps, because its plotting makes Grandcourt's loss of life Gwendolyn's gain?) On the one hand, Gwendolyn is placed in the position – that of Madame Laure in *Middlemarch* – of the actress who enacts the madness that comes from a devotion to self-display by murdering her husband. At the very least, by offering no extenuating commentary on the scene, and by skirting, so awkwardly, the question of accountability, Eliot's novel lets a kind of guiltiness attach to Gwendolyn. On the other hand, Deronda, the novel's moral authority, is made to come to Gwendolyn's defense. In defending her, Deronda deploys the very religious discourse that the novel has, in relation to Gwendolyn, gradually undermined, as when he reflects that Gwendolyn's "remorse was the precious sign of a recoverable nature; it was the culmination of that self-disapproval which had been the awakening of a new life within her" (762). In a decisive, authoritative speech, Deronda dismisses the notion of making her story public, and then goes on to allay Gwendolyn's fear that her "murderous will" might, even indirectly, be the cause of Grandcourt's death:

"No – I think not," said Deronda slowly. "If it were true that he could swim, he must have been seized with cramp. With your quickest, utmost effort, it seems impossible that you could have done anything to save him. That momentary murderous will cannot, I think, have altered the course of events. Its effect is confined to the motives in your own breast." (764)

One has to step back for a moment to see that Deronda's reassuring conclusion fellows logically from a premise that is mere hypothesis: "if it were true that he could swim." *Deronda* itself doesn't tell us whether or not Grandcourt could swim, choosing, on this point, to deny its own omniscience. Deronda goes on to discuss the rabbinical *yezer hara*, the evil will in its internal and external manifestations, as if theological discourse were most appropriate to the occasion. Religious concerns displace legal, but only after Deronda absolves Gwendolyn of guilt on conjectural, not representational, grounds.

At this moment in *Deronda*, the significance of Gwendolyn's leaping into the sea is suddenly open to interpretation in a way that foreshadows Conrad's *Lord Jim*. But, simultaneously,

Deronda parts company with his predecessors, for whom representation is inseparable from fidelity to respectably bourgeois
conceptions of justice. Gwendolyn can breathe a sigh of relief
once she's received Deronda's absolution, but *Deronda*'s readers,
who hang as eagerly on Deronda's words as she does, remain in
doubt. It doesn't help that Deronda has a habit of trimming his
words to the needs of his auditors. When Gwendolyn earlier asks
what prevented Mirah from drowning herself in despair, Deronda
responds, vaguely, "Some ray or other came – which made her
feel that she ought to live – that it was good to live"; and Mordecai is told nothing at all (494). The novel has consistently emphasized the psychological need Deronda has to protect others.
"Persons attracted him," we are told, "in proportion to the possibility of his defending them, rescuing them, telling upon their
lives with some sort of redeeming influence" (369). Though
Deronda doesn't rescue Gwendolyn, as we've seen, he certainly
defends and influences her. In stressing his need to do so,
however, *Deronda* makes its hero's intervention in the scene of
death by drowning as problematical as its own wishful attempt
to make development a spiritual affair. Departing, with visionary
foresight, from objectivist views of truth, in an uneasy transforming process, *Deronda* dissolves the marriage of bourgeois
rationality and ethico-psychological realism from which mentorship in earlier texts had drawn its strength.

5

The authority of moral discourse, a staple of bourgeois realism
Deronda puts at risk, is much more seriously compromised by
Wharton's *The House of Mirth*. As has already been mentioned, the
novels are interconnected in a number of ways, *Deronda* perhaps
having influenced even the coincidental meeting up of the hero
and heroine-in-distress while on holiday in the Mediterranean.
The fact that both heroines, given to controlled self-display,
appear in *tableaux vivants* is one of the significant points of connection to have received critical attention. Just as important,
though, is the class-inflected love of luxury and ease that they
share. Gwendolyn's hatred of "hardships, ugliness and humilia-

tion" sparks Lily's equally passionate disdain for – her mother's word – "dinginess." *Deronda* opens with Gwendolyn at the gambling tables, and Lily loses badly at bridge when at Bellomont, her destiny when we first meet her. Gambling, a sign of moral bankruptcy in bourgeois fiction, plays a special role in these novels, for the heroine desperately needs money if she is to retain her ornamental status. In both, gambling is also associated with a peculiarity of the heroine's psychology, her tendency to leave major decisions up to chance, which, in practice, means letting impulses of the moment overrule conscious intentions. Impulsiveness, besides characterizing Gwendolyn, fuels the drinking, gambling, and stealing of *Deronda*'s downwardly mobile Lapidoth. As if taking this in a direction appropriate to the growing consumerism of early twentieth-century America, Wharton makes addiction a controlling figure in *Mirth*, where Lily's "craving for the external finish of life" compels most of her decisions, and the overdose that ends her life satisfies "her physical craving for sleep" (I, 3, 22; II, 13, 250).

The male rake's female counterpart is, of course, the prostitute, an identity both Gwendolyn and Lily come perilously close to assuming. Called in to advise Gwendolyn of her chances at making her living as an actress, Klesmer hints that unless she submits to the discipline of becoming a real artist, she might end up using the stage merely as a means of selling herself. When Gwendolyn escapes the indignity of being a governess by marrying, she becomes a wife only ambiguously, Grandcourt, as she knows, already being as good as married, though he refuses to give legal sanction to the long-standing union with Lydia Glasher that has produced four children. Grandcaurt's will, which makes their son his heir, not only punishes Gwendolyn for failing to produce a child but turns her, publicly, into his kept woman. Part of Grandcourt's power over Gwendolyn comes from his ability to induce shame, which has a sexual coloring whenever she thinks about the awkwardness a possible separation from Grandcourt might create in her relations with Deronda: "instinctively she felt that the separation would be from him too, and in the prospective vision of herself as a solitary, dubiously regarded woman she felt some tingling bashfulness at the remembrance of her

behaviour towards him" (666). After her self-revealing appearance in the *tableaux vivants* Lily becomes the object of discussion among men, where she is passed around, verbally, with contempt. An aggrieved cousin refers to her "standing there as if she was up at auction," while Ned Van Alstyne points to the danger courted by "the young woman who claims the privileges of marriage without assuming its obligations" (I, 14, 124). In her encounter with Gus Trenor, whose demands for a return on the money he's given her threaten to include rape, Lily is overwhelmed by waves of an intensely sexualized shame, and later, having fled to Gerty, imagines confessing to Selden, "I've sunk lower than the lowest, for I've taken what they take, and not paid as they pay" (I, 14, 132).

In *Vindication*, Wollstonecraft objects to the expectation that women "supinely dream life away in the *lap* of pleasure, or the languor of weariness" (my italics) (112). More than once, Wollstonecraft compares women to pet spaniels, a comparison Eliot uses when – in one of her more scathing put-downs – Gwendolyn is likened to a "lap-dog" (*Vindication*, 179; *Deronda*, 607). A debased, sexualized femininity is associated with the enervating lap of pleasure in *Mirth*, as well, when Lily, in her graduated fall, takes pleasure in the luxury offered by the shady Emporium Hotel, where she is "once more lapped and folded in ease" (II, 9, 212). Lily is in every way the creature of sensation Wollstonecraft laments. Specifically consumerist drives make her very much the product of the historical period in which Wharton writes, however. That Lily, who can't afford it, spends all her money – including the $9,000 given her by Trenor – on clothes and jewelry would have rung a warning bell for readers of Wharton's time. As *Sister Carrie* demonstrates, an uncontrolled passion for dress both signifies and inexorably leads to the breaking through of other forms of womanly restraint. The medical and scientific discourse of the time promoted the view that female "vanity" and "the love of finery" are actually the main factors *causing* prostitution. Like the lower-class women who are the objects of this discourse, the unmarried Lily wears a style of clothing only upper-class wives can afford (and like the servants who are berated for doing so, Lily wears Mrs. Trenor's hand-me-downs).[26]

As much as her love of luxury, then, Lily's love of "finery" (a word Wharton uses) places her on a dangerous downward course.

In *Writing*, Wharton qualifies her very high praise of George Eliot ("perhaps born with the richest gifts of any English novelist since Thackeray") because her writing was affected by the "tidal wave of prudery" that washed over the English novel around the time of Scott. Had it not been for this, Wharton says, Eliot "might have poured out her treasures of wit and irony and tenderness without continually pausing to denounce and exhort."[27] Eliot's moralizing – aiding and abetting a real conservatism – is especially grating in *Deronda*'s references to marriage (an institution Eliot entered only shortly before her death). *Deronda* views marriage as an unproblematical, gender-neutral contract, claiming, for example, that "all the ostensible advantages" are on Gwendolyn's side in the contract she has with Grandcourt. When Gwendolyn struggles with the question of separation, the narrator (in a gross display of moralism) says "her capability of rectitude told her again and again that she had no right to complain of her contract, or to withdraw from it." Traces of the chivalric code articulated in *Grandison*'s defence of patriarchal relations appear in Deronda's reflection that "as Mirah's betrothed husband he would gain a protective authority." When he proposes marriage to Mirah, the narrator responds, piously, "Deronda was giving her the highest tribute man can give to woman"(732, 665, 857, 863).

This looks very much like mystification from the vantage point of Wharton's *Mirth*, with its thoroughgoing send-up of marriage, at least as practiced by the upper classes. In the society Lily inhabits, marriage is viewed exclusively as an economic arrangement, the only extra-economic feature being the protection it offers women for their extramarital affairs – and that is clearly a matter of tacit social convention, not of chivalry or contract: "The code of Lily's world decreed that a woman's husband should be the only judge of her conduct; she was technically above suspicion while she had the shelter of his approval, or even of his indifference" (I, 9, 82).[28] Even divorce, a ready option for this class, can be economically motivated, as Mrs. Fisher's case shows.

It's not only Eliot's prudery that Wharton backs away from in *Mirth*, though, but her spirituality and idealism as well. The nasty, gratuitous anti-Semitism conveyed in the portrait of Rosedale – a parvenu appearing elsewhere in Wharton as a white Protestant – signals, right away, that *Mirth* is stubbornly determined to resist *Deronda*'s intensely motivated polemic, regarded, it would seem, as smacking too much of missionary zeal.

In *Deronda*, the language of religion – references to Gwendolyn's conscience, conversion, her purgatory, regeneration – comes to have a contradictory relation to the strong inertial force of what Eliot calls Gwendolyn's "egotism." There is no such tension in *Mirth*, which constructs Lily's self-destructive tendencies as fixed psychological patterns. Their static, predictable quality imparts an almost Racinian clarity to the trajectory of Lily's fall. With a strongly naturalist emphasis, the opening chapter positions Lily as the product of social and economic forces. As Lily falls, psychological patterns that have already been dramatized for us are precisely described, thereby taking on an almost equally determining externality. Two of the patterns turned by verbal fiat into psychic laws involve both self-deception and an uncannily ruinous sense of timing. The first, demonstrated in the Gryce affair, has Lily at the last minute throwing away a chance to marry, after she's marshaled all her arts to obtain it. The second, first shown us in the transaction with Trenor, is summed up by the narrator as Lily's habit of withdrawing "from an ambiguous situation in time to save her self-respect, but too late for public vindication" (II, 10, 221). In her pursuit of pleasure, Lily gives this particular pattern plenty of chances to repeat itself, which is how *Mirth* indicates that Lily is incapable of "renewal," her addictive love of her old ways being much more powerful than any stray desire to reform.

The rigidities of the novel's naturalism are offset by the hopes aroused by Selden's mentorship, however. By positioning Selden as a mentor, *Mirth* puts in play the entire set of expectations his role conventionally encourages. We are led to hope – against hope – that Selden will rescue Lily from herself, that she will leave behind her frivolous ways, forswear getting and spending, and join Selden in a life of modest but elegant domesticity. Like his predecessors, Selden possesses the superior rationality of bourgeois man, which enables him to assess with precision the "crudeness" of Lily's preferences. In the aura of learning and distinction he communicates, Selden is especially close to Deronda. As if to underline the connection between male mentorship and learning, both *Deronda* and *Mirth* arrange encounters in libraries inhabited by the heroes. In response to one of Gwendolyn's appeals, Deronda exhorts her to take refuge from her "personal trouble" in "the higher, the religious life" (506). The more resolutely secular *Mirth* has Selden offer Lily membership in "the republic of the spirit" (I, 6, 55, 56). In both novels, the reader is made to hope that with the aid of her mentor the heroine will raise herself, will transcend her debased femininity and enter his promised land.

When speaking with her mentor, Lily, like Gwendolyn, falls into an uncharacteristically direct, self-revealing manner. In both novels, the absence of "coquetry" is explicitly commented upon, as if the heroine is able to dispense with a disabling femininity only when under her mentor's spell. But if the mentor's plain spoken style is masculine, the heroine's is plaintively childlike. *Mirth*, like *Deronda*, presents the heroine's radical defenselessness through the narrative equivalent of stage direction, as in the scene in the Brys conservatory: "Suddenly she raised her eyes with the beseeching earnestness of a child. 'You never speak to me – you think – hard things of me,' she murmured" (I, 15, 137). As children, however, Gwendolyn and Lily are definitely *bad* children. The effect on Gwendolyn of being with Deronda is "to be roused into self-judgment" (508). Through the standard he sets, she is brought to see herself as "selfish and ignorant" – though Deronda states, categorically, "You will not go on being selfish and ignorant" (502). Lily tells Selden he's ruined her self-respect, and when he responds caustically, in a way expressing disapproval, Wharton writes, "She looked at him helplessly, like a hurt or frightened child: this real self of hers, which he had the faculty of drawing out of the depths, was so little accustomed to go alone!" (I, 8, 75)

For both heroines, intense need of the mentor's approval can trigger either further self-blame or the desire to please. Toward the end of both novels, an overwhelming sense of gratitude expresses itself in an agony of self-abasement. Intense, emotionally charged scenes reveal the triumph of the irrepressible and redeemable "child" over the polished demeanor of the female rake. After Grandcourt's drowning, *Deronda* has: " 'You have saved me from worse,' said Gwendolyn, in a sobbing voice. 'I should have been worse, if it had not been for you. If you had not been good, I should have been more wicked than I am' " (767). Later, in the separation scene, she says, through her sobs, "I said . . . I said . . . it should be better . . . better with me . . . for having known you" (878). A similar confession bursts forth from Lily in her last meeting with Selden, when she tells him that "I have never forgotten the things you said to me at Bellomont, and that sometimes – sometimes when I seemed farthest from remembering them – they have helped me, and kept me from mistakes; kept me from really becoming what many people have thought me" (II, 12, 239). Although Lily doesn't sob, tears finally interrupt the long speech in which she tells Selden how much strength his vision has given her: "That is what you did for me – that is what I wanted to thank you for. I wanted to tell you that I have always remembered; and that I have tried – tried hard . . ." (II, 12, 240).

These scenes, however, consummate (so to speak) the mentor–protégée relationship, which begins in the externality of the gaze. *Mirth* opens exactly as *Deronda* does, with the mentor looking upon the heroine as he muses on the meaning of her beauty. Through the mentor's male gaze, both heroines are constituted as objects of scrutiny and for control.[29] But where in *Deronda* the prospective mentor reflects on the ambiguities of the heroine's moral character, *Mirth* opens with the statement that Selden's "eyes had been refreshed by the sight of Lily Bart" – "refreshed" being quite as loaded as the "vex" that appears in the opening sentence of *Emma*. Spectatorship – associated with the idle "speculation" on which Wharton puns – is thematized by *Mirth* in its indictment of the new, consumerist society. But Selden's ability to distance himself emotionally also expresses his highly developed aesthetic taste, the fastidiousness of which draws Lily to him. (For readers of *Deronda* and *Portrait*, this signals trouble, since fastidiousness is exactly what attracts Gwendolyn to the passionless Grandcourt and Isabel to the equally abusive Osmond, Grandcourt's heir.)

Deronda introduces a new element into the mentor tradition by almost completely psychologizing its hero's "chivalrous sentiment" (247). The pain of illegitimacy together with a protective attitude toward his absent mother create in Deronda a need to rescue others, to be of service, especially to women. Although neither Sir Charles nor Mr. Knightley is infallible, the guidance they offer belongs to a chivalrous rationality that transcends the merely personal. Both *Grandison* and *Emma* recognize that to subjectivize the mentor's role would be to call that extrapersonal order into question. As we've seen, this is just what happens when, in the crisis at Genoa, Deronda gets its mentor to save the heroine's self-esteem at the expense of representing what actually happened. James, responding to *Deronda*, psychologizes his mentor, too. But mentorship is also ironized in *Portrait*, where Touchett, motivated by a desire to keep Isabel to himself so he can live through her, pressures his father into giving her part of his inheritance – an intervention indirectly responsible for Isabel's fall. By far the most important influence *Portrait* has on *Mirth*, this ironization of mentorship comes at the end of a tradition originating in preindustrial capitalism, and seems to indicate the breakdown of patriarchal forms not servicable in the new consumer age.

Although he, too, is psychologized, Selden is a more full-blooded descendent of his chivalrous predecessors than is Touchett. Like Knightley in relation to Jane Fairfax and Miss Bates, Selden thoughtfully arranges transportation for the unprotected Gerty Farish. True to his brothers in mentorship, Selden responds to appeals for help and tries to protect the honor of his charge, as when he aids and advises Lily after she's been publicly shamed by Mrs. Dorset. Whenever Selden shows his solidarity with his fellow mentors, the expectation that Lily might come around is raised. Yet after the crisis of faith that causes him to break off with her, even this expectation is ringed with irony. For in Book II Selden seems to use the role of Lily's mentor as a means of distancing himself emotionally. All good mentors know they must risk offending or alienating their protégées. As Knightley says to Emma, it's not at all pleasant to have to tell her "truths," but he must be "satisfied with proving myself your friend by very faithful counsel, and trusting that you will some time or other do me greater justice than you can do now" (368). But when Selden acts on this principle by confronting Lily about her position with Mrs. Hatch, he does so as if obeying only its letter. Because his actions have already communicated a lack of trust, Lily proudly resists every word he says. And Selden, equally defensive, masks his own feelings by appealing formally to the privileges patriarchy has assigned him. His "right" to suggest that Lily remove herself "is simply the *universal* right of a man to enlighten a woman when he sees her unconsciously placed in a false position" (my italics) (II, 9, 218).

What gives *Mirth* its suspenseful, tautly balanced dramatic tension is the perpetual, ever-renewed conflict between the expectations raised by Selden's mentorship and their persistant, ironic disappointment. Bad timing plays an important role in sustaining the tension, and in giving it an impersonal, tragic character. Although associated primarily with Lily, mistiming increasingly becomes a feature of Selden's interventions, with the result that it gradually also assumes an *inter*personal character. In every one of their exchanges something is held back, not said, not risked or given, so that at the very moment it arises an opportunity for commitment or clarification is passed by. In the novel's love scenes there is an uneasy atmosphere of illicitness, as there is in *Deronda*. In *Mirth*, however, any potential adulterousness is purely hypothetical, having reference only to the wealthy husband Lily is engaged, half-heartedly, in seeking. That Lily is as good as betrothed – that she must remain faithful to her destiny as a wealthy wife – is a fiction Lily and Seldon both accept, for it protects them from having to take seriously the possibility of their being in love. This possibility is there – creating a heady excitement in the first scene and a kiss in the second – but it coexists with a strong sense of unreality, the product of their mutual self-protectiveness.

Retrospectively, for the reader, though, it's this very pact that makes the illicitness. By mutual agreement, their one-on-one meetings turn out to have no purchase on reality. It's almost, strangely, as if their meetings hadn't happened, so powerful are the mechanisms of denial at work. Moments of intimacy, ripe with possibility, are followed by what seems almost a kind of amnesia. This rhythm, which characterizes their meetings in Book I, has a counterpart in each character's psychic process. We are told, early on, that Lily's "whole being dilated in an atmosphere of luxury" (I, 3, 23), and are then presented with a scene in which her imagination basks in the pleasure of anticipating her future as Mrs. Gryce. Lily's leisurely internal enjoyment of her future arises from a premature sense of achievement, which Selden's presence soon makes her want to devalue and destroy. Narcissistic dilation followed by failure and/or a reaction of self-disgust is the rhythm to which Lily falls. Accompanying it is the forgetting that succeeds her moments of intimacy with Selden, which have a similarly provisional, aesthetically pleasing plenitude.

In the novel's crisis, Selden's psyche is governed by the same dynamic. On the wings of love and a hoped-for marriage, Selden goes to Mrs. Fisher's in the hope of joining Lily, who has just left. In her absence she has become a vulgarly sexual object of verbal exchange, highly threatening to Selden's internal image of her, which is radically aesthetic. Lily's performance at the Brys' entertainment strikes him as revealing the "real Lily Bart, divested of the trivialities of her little world, and catching for a moment a note of that eternal harmony of which her beauty was a part" (I, 12, 106). At Mrs. Fisher's, where this idealized aesthetic object comes into contact with the contaminating words of mortal men, Selden comes to its imaginary defense by fantasizing upon the deliverance he will offer:

It was her element, not his. But he would lift her out of it, take her beyond! That *Beyond!* on her letter was like a cry for rescue. He knew that Perseus' task is not done when he has loosed Andromeda's chains, for her limbs are numb with bondage, and she cannot rise and walk, but clings to him with dragging arms as he beats back to land with his burden. Well, he had strength for both – it was her weakness which had put the strength in him. (I, 14, 125)

90

Within a matter of only minutes, Selden has forgotten these high-flown heroic intentions, however. When Lily leaves Gus Trenor's house just as he and Van Alstyne happen by, Selden actually *sees* her as a fallen woman. So strongly influenced is he by the society he claims to despise that the incarnation of ideal beauty perceptible only to his enlightened eyes, the Andromeda in need of Perseus's rescue, appears, unexpectedly, as a kind of tramp – her stock having suddenly crashed.

Mirth thoroughly ironizes the convention that the mentor rescue the heroine so that she can love. In the Brys conservatory love scene, Selden responds to Lily's appeal for help with, "The only way I can help you is by loving you" (I, 12, 109). Instead of letting it die on his lips, Selden plans to make this into a formal proposal two days later. The first irony of the novel's crisis at the end of Book I is that had Selden actually made this proposal, Lily would have accepted it – only, however, because in the shame and desperation that engulf her after meeting with Trenor she finally finds "a promise of rescue in [Selden's] love" (I, 15, 138). By far the greater irony is that just when Lily eagerly awaits this rescue, Selden refuses to offer it on grounds that completely undermine his role as mentor. For by leaping, immediately, to the conclusion most damaging to Lily, Selden betrays one of the major duties of mentorship, which is the offering of constant, unwavering belief (amounting to love) that the heroine is not her outward, false self – that her better self will eventually emerge. Deronda denies that Gwendolyn's murderous will is guilty of anything, even though Grandcourt lies there dead. Sex, not murder, is the issue in *Mirth*, but though Lily is, like Gwendolyn, deeply implicated, the reader knows for sure that she isn't Trenor's mistress. By maintaining representational authority over Lily's relations with Trenor, *Mirth* puts Selden in the position of being, simply, mistaken in what he suspects. Although Selden, like Deronda, ends up in the Mediterranean area, he leaves New York for the same reason Gwendolyn flees for the Leubronn: to avoid a compromising marriage. The connection, again, works ironically, for Grandcourt does in fact have another sexual partner, whereas Lily's is only the product of Selden's imagination.

In doubting Lily, Selden loses his authority as rational man and steps out of his hero-as-mentor part. But *Mirth* wants us to see more than this, as is evident from the story Nettle Struther tells of being loved by the man now her husband in spite of her earlier involvement with a "gentleman" who had deceived her. Even if Lily *had* been Trenor's mistress, Selden's response would have had no moral foundation, since it assumes the sexual double standard *Mirth* wants to problematize. As we've seen, in *Grandison* and *Deronda* the hero enjoys the privileges of the sexual double standard, but because the male mentor is, above all, virtuous, the double standard operates only in a rarified, spiritual sphere: both men are without sexual experience before they marry (Grandison actually discusses this). *Mirth*, perhaps a bit impatient with the prudery of this bourgeois Protestant tradition, boldly presents us with a mentor who ends an affair with a married woman, Bertha Dorset, shortly before the novel's action begins. This isn't merely a technical innovation, however, for it opens up perspectives and ironies that are specifically feminist. The first novel in the mentor tradition to expose the sexism of the double standard, *Mirth* has its hero rely on it in a way that thoroughly sabotages his mentorship. Were Lily to have had an affair with the married Gus Trenor, she would have duplicated exactly Selden's experience. As it is, however, the sexually experienced Selden deserts Lily the moment he suspects her of having an affair, while, despite the signs of depravity attaching to her as she falls, Lily dies as untouched, symbolically, as the flower whose name she bears.

The overturning of chivalrous rescue by the sexual double standard becomes *Mirth*'s central, ironic, organizing conceit. When Mrs. Haffen confronts Lily with the letters from Mrs. Dorset she finds at Selden's, Lily decides to buy them in order to protect Selden, feeling, instinctively, that he would want the letters "rescued." As is explicitly mentioned, Selden is already protected by the double standard, but Lily fears that Mrs. Haffen's discovery of the correspondence "would convict Selden of negligence in a matter where the world holds it least pardonable" (I, 9, 83). Lily herself, though, is guilty of nothing more substantial than "negligence." The faulty parallelism is worked out exactly:

Lily, knowing Selden to have had an affair with Mrs. Dorset, chivalrously acts to protect him from the incidental charge of negligence, while Selden fails to protect Lily from this very charge because he wrongly suspects that she is guilty of something worse. The ironies of this situation, intensified throughout by Selden's playing at mentor, are still there in the closing scenes. On her way to blackmail Bertha Dorset, Lily "seemed suddenly to see her action as [Selden] would see it," and is moved by shame and longing to visit him (II, 11, 237). Once in Selden's presence and feeling the full force of her love, Lily burns the letters instead of using them to her own advantage as she had planned: she continues to protect Selden as well as her love for him. By contrast, when Selden, in Lily's room after her death, discovers the envelope addressed to Trenor, he reacts with the full force of all his earlier doubts, his very memories suddenly feeling contaminated.

Neither character knows anything of the other's thoughts or actions, however. Only the reader knows what's really going on, a feature of *Mirth* that makes it, in part, a tragedy of mistiming and miscommunication. In the novel's crisis, three characters come to disillusionment on the very same night – Lily with herself, Selden with her, and Gerty with Selden – but in spite of their interrelations, each suffers in total silence. The absence of openness is a function of the alienation built into the society of surfaces that *Mirth* satirizes, while the emphasis on timing gestures toward the impersonality of the structures that govern fates, an impersonality exemplified by the market's inexplicable rises and crashes. *Mirth*'s tragic mode tends to apportion blame equally between Selden and Lily. They are both presented as victims of society who equally resist the trust and frankness that could have united them. As formal proof, in the concluding chapters each takes responsibility for having rejected the offer of love (though Lily wrongly thinks it was the third trial that was too much for Selden); and each comes, too late, upon the "word" that would clarify all.

Although for a brief moment it looks as if it might be, this isn't *Romeo and Juliet*, however. The ironies attending the subversion of mentorship end up tipping the balanced scales of tragedy. In

Book II, Lily's graduated fall, which makes her increasingly vulnerable and desperate, causes Selden to appear almost smugly self-protective. The pathos of their last meeting is all on Lily's side, in part because once again we know what Selden doesn't. Having kept his distance, Selden actually knows very little – less then Rosedale, ironically, to whom Lily, eager to clear herself, explains the whole Trenor episode. Eliot's mentor knows that under other circumstances he would have loved Gwendolyn, and as he steels himself for their separation, we're told that had it not been for his commitment to Mirah, Deronda's unreflective instinct would have been "to save her from sorrow, to shelter her life for evermore from the dangers of loneliness, and carry out to the last the rescue he had begun in that monitory redemption of the necklace" (835). Touchett, too, says he might have loved Isabel had things been different; but this hypothetical sentiment isn't returned, and rescue and romance are reserved for other characters.

Mirth brings romance, rescue, marriage, and mentorship back together again – only to have Selden decline the passion that would bind them. At the end of Book I, Selden withholds his offer of marriage; at the end of Book II he goes to make it after Lily is dead. Selden as good as abandons Lily in their last meeting, though he doesn't know it. Lacking Deronda's tremendous empathic capacity, and being, besides, ignorant of Lily's real state, Selden isn't involved in her suffering. The concluding paragraphs of *Mirth*, presenting his response to Lily's death, place him permanently beyond the reach of Lily's pain. Once he's pieced together the story of Lily's financial transaction with Trenor, Selden is so elated at the recovery of his belief in her that he passes rapidly into a state of self-consolation, from which their separation by death comes to seem reassuringly inevitable. Narcissistic plenitude here works to distance Selden emotionally from both self-reproach and loss. There *is* no loss, really, for he feels Lily's death has made it possible for them to save the moment of their love "whole." The pure virtuality of this moment of love gives it an aesthetic quality that protects it, granting it a commoditylike autonomy and fixity. In its aura, Selden can rewrite the past, giving his "faith" in Lily the very constancy that would have befit a mentor in love.

The increasing pathos of Lily's situation, where loss is manifold and real, is part and parcel of a process of enoblement that doesn't extend to Selden, who becomes ever more definitely an antihero. Both *Deronda* and *Mirth* progressively increase their heroines' stature by using language suggesting nobility. *Mirth* also shows Lily to be more and more opposed to all forms of compromise, open to new feelings, and concerned with issues that seem moral. We are told that "there had been nothing in her training to develop any continuity of moral strength" (II, 8, 204). And yet *Mirth* gives Lily something like this strength when resisting temptation. "Temptation" is the term used by *Mirth* in Book II, which dramatically structures the proposals of marriage made Lily by Dorset and Rosedale as temptation ordeals.

In Book I, it's "a smothered sense of resistance" that sparks Lily's revolt against churchgoing as a means of catching Gryce (I, 5, 47). As with Gwendolyn, Lily's resistance can express the rebellious impulses of a dissatisfied, passionately unruly self. Even after she's denied the legacy she counted on, this resistant self declares, "For I'm absolutely impenitent, you know," following on the narrator's, "She drew herself up to the full height of her slender majesty, towering like some dark angel of defiance above the troubled Gerty" (II, 4, 176). This rebellious, Romantic resistance is not what compels her to resist Dorset's and Rosedale's proposals of marriage, however. Resistance to temptation (constructed by *Mirth* precisely to display this) expresses the exquisite fineness of her sensibilities. Earlier, when Mrs. Gaffen tries to blackmail her, Lily's horror expresses "all her instinctive resistances, of taste, of training, of blind inherited scruples" (I, 9, 82). The word "inherited" appears frequently in *Mirth*, always suggesting values more genuine than those manufactured by the nourveau riche. *The Decoration of Houses*, Wharton's first work, relies on a similar distinction, revealing Wharton's allegiance to her own upper-class origins. Rosedale, a newcomer to Lily's society, admires Lily even more after she resists the ingenious proposal he outlines, the reason being that "the sense in her of unexplained scruples and resistances had the same attraction as the delicacy of feature, the fastidiousness of manner, which gave her an external rarity, an air of being impossible to match" (II, 11, 234).

As this analogy makes clear, instinctive resistances and blind inherited scruples are hardly the same thing as moral convictions. Yet when the narrator talks of Lily's having no "continuity of moral strength," reference is made to "her intermittent impulses of resistance," leaving open the possibility that a steadfast practice of resistance might be equivalent to moral strength. Like Selden's, Lily's idealism and aestheticism are viewed ironically. Yet *Mirth* ironizes Lily's superiority only up to a certain point, beyond which she stands forth as the real thing. In resisting the terms of a materialistic world of commerce and surface, Lily becomes a genuine heroine in the second part of Wharton's novel – but a heroine who is, above all, a lady. Although *Mirth* can be hard on Lily, it doesn't ever suggest that ethical principles are categorically distinct from the essentially aesthetic form taken by her scruples. Caught between emergent consumer capitalism and an ineffectual, outmoded gentility, *Mirth*'s moral codes are fundamentally unstable, the scruples and fastidiousness of true gentility having to represent (having been exchanged for) moral continuity.

Lily's resistance can pass for principled because the values she protects – even at the cost of her life – are, for the realist novel, highly conventional. The proposals she receives take the form of temptations because they turn marriage into a bargain. By refusing to enter into negotiations, Lily protects the bourgeois ideal of marriage for love. When she resists Rosedale's proposal, she does so seeing "that the essential baseness of the act lay in its freedom from risk" (II, 7, 203). Lily's commitment to "risk" shows her sharing in the market mentality of her society. But what she really objects to is Rosedale's attempt to buy her trust, for it means the complete absence of emotional risk – the closest thing to love in the marriage Rosedale proposes. By protecting, even in such a displaced form, the ideal of romantic love, Lily also, indirectly, defends her chastity. Refusing to sell herself not only once but repeatedly, Lily gradually undoes the sexualized effects of her fall. In her last visit with Selden, Lily gives up not only marriage with Rosedale but the part of herself that was willing even to consider economically advantageous proposals such as his. With this renunciation, Lily becomes a virtuous heroine, symbolically attaining a state of sexual-emotional purity. When Lily destroys Mrs. Dorset's letters, she destroys the hard, money-bitten Lily, always potentially a prostitute. The act is complexly overdetermined, for in closing off the possibility of bargaining with the letters, Lily protects not only Selden but also, and perhaps most significantly, the chaste Lily, who has learned, finally, the meaning of true love: "the passion of her soul for his" (II, 12, 241).

In addition, by this act Lily protects the woman who has helped to ruin her. Initially, Lily is quite as willing as Bertha Dorset to play dirty. At Bellomont, Lily pretends to an engage-ment with Selden in the same spirit of gratuitously nasty female rivalry that governs Bertha Dorset's actions throughout. Since *Mirth* requires that Lily become, eventually, a proper heroine, though, she cleans up her act in Book II. Her loyalty to Bertha Dorset makes her superior to her rival, whose untrustworthiness is made obvious to the reader. Ignorance of evil, a touching but misplaced trust – these are highly conventioinal characteristics of the virtuous bourgeois heroine whose innocence unfits her for the mean, monied world we know. Lily's ultimate triumph over her desire to take revenge on Mrs. Dorset establishes her sisterly solidarity with earlier heroines such as Richardson's Pamela, Harriet, and Clementina. It sits oddly, however, with *Mirth's* emphasis on the emptiness and viciousness of female relations. Since Austen, the realist novel had come to include jealousy and rivalry in its depiction of female-female relations. Even the sick-eningly good Mirah experiences jealousy of Gwendolyn. And the perfectly virtuous Gerty (modeled on *Middlemarch's* Mary Garth) has to struggle with envy of Lily. But *Mirth* goes beyond any of its predecessors in its portrayal of a war of woman against woman. With only a couple of exceptions, relations among women are stripped bare of any and all protective idealism.

Mirth's satiric spirit has this corrosive effect on every aspect of society it touches. Its cost seems too great, however, for a kind of backlash seems evident in the concluding chapters. Nostalgia informs the triumph in Lily of "inherited" forms. Nettie Struthers's domestic haven is a product of the same *embourgeoisement* of the proletariat as can be found in Engels's *The Origin of the Family, Private Property and the State*, though Wharton seems to have gone to Dickens for the sentimentalism of the scene. Further, when before she dies Lily feels "the clutch of solitude at her heart," the narrator emphasizes her essential rootlessness in language that recalls a similar passage in *Deronda*. Like Gwendolyn, Lily grew up without "any one spot of earth being dearer to her than another; there was no centre of early pieties, of grave endearing traditions, to which her heart could revert and from which it could draw strength for itself and tenderness for others" (II, 13, 248).[30] The related passage in *Deronda* appears early on in "The Spoiled Child," where the influences determining Gwendolyn are being presented (50). When it appears at the very end of *Mirth*, however, the passage seems to serve only rhetorical ends. Heightening the pathos of Lily's situation, it becomes part of the novel's unstable, ungrounded sentimentalization of the past.

Yet even *Deronda*'s talk of roots seems *awkwardly* nostalgic, as if Eliot is importing sentiments from *The Mill on the Floss* and *Middlemarch* into the restless, cosmopolitan scene of her last novel. Restlessness, discontinuity, and forgetting are integral to *Mirth*, which seems to anticipate the technique of rapid scene shifting later developed by television and film. When Wharton seizes desperately, at the last minute, on Eliot's voice, the result isn't, then, exactly reassuring, for the intertext doesn't really belong to *Mirth*'s society of consumer capitalism. In *Deronda*, the mentor's belief in the heroine's potentially good self is the only thing Gwendolyn finally has to hang onto. *Mirth*, too, leaves its heroine with only "the uplifting memory of [Selden's] faith in her" (II, 13, 249). The uplifting *fiction* of his faith in her would be more accurate, however, since the chastened, repentant Lily bestows much more, imaginatively, on her mentor than he does on her. At the end of their last meeting, Lily touches Selden's forehead with her lips, a gesture carefully imitating Maggie Tulliver's dignified, almost maternal, farewell kissing of Phillip Wakem.

With this, the heroine of *The Mill on the Floss* – a text brimful with nostalgia – enters Lily Bart, making her death, too, signal the loss of a spirit too complex, too noble for the crassly materialist world that's failed to understand.

In concluding, I'd like to reflect, briefly, on some patterns and endings. When Lydia Glasher confronts her at the Whispering Stones, Gwendolyn feels "a sort of terror: it was as if some ghastly vision had come to her in a dream and said, 'I am a woman's life'" (190). In fleeing this Gothic scene, Gwendolyn is, of course, overtaken by the fate she fears: like Lily she ends up living, with a vengeance, a woman's life. What Touchett says of the defeated Isabel therefore applies to Gwendolyn and Lily, too: "[Y]ou were punished for your wish. You were ground in the very mill of the conventional."[31] In *Emma*, *Deronda*, and *Mirth*, mentor and author alike are complicit in the heroine's punishment, at least at the level of the normative discourse on femininity each novel articulates. All three novels express something of the aggressivity of Wollstonecraft's *Vindication* in plotting to reduce their rakish heroines to tears. In part, as we've seen, this aggressivity is directed against femininity's narcissistic love of pleasure. But it's also directed against the desire to *resist* certain aspects of femininity, the ideology of romantic love and, implicitly, motherhood, for Emma, Gwendolyn, and Lily all act out (though with much less conviction than the Alcarisi) a "wish" to reject, out of hand, a woman's life. Might this more disturbing assault – certainly not to be found in *Vindication* – be motivated by a punitive internalization of patriarchal values? Catherine Gallagher has argued that in nineteenth-century England the woman who published her writing in exchange for money took on, metaphorically, the identity of whore.[32] Perhaps it's not surprising, then, that, though Austen, Eliot, and Wharton all successfully resist living a woman's life, their heroines – whose longing for freedom isn't nearly so productive – don't 'scape grinding in the very mill of the conventional.

Yet because the heroine's wish goes unfulfilled, these texts also at the same time express, however problematically, a utopian demand. In *Emma* this demand is more or less met by the heightened, romantic glow cast by the tensely dramatic proposal scene appearing toward its close. As with most of Austen's novels, idealization of the marriage soon to be celebrated sets to rest doubts that were earlier entertained. By marrying her mentor, Emma follows the "Oedipal" script written for white women in industrialized, Euro-American societies. (To counter associations of incest, Knightley – who's more than fifteen years Emma's senior and has cared for her since she was a child – agrees to move into the Woodhouse home after their marriage.) In *Deronda* and *Mirth*, however, where relations with the male mentor are *so deeply troubled*, it's "pre-Oedipal" desires that get fulfilled. As was mentioned earlier, pre-Oedipal desires are frequently indulged in contemporary mass-produced romance. But in popular romance the longing to return to the mother is satisfied only in the guise of union with a strongly phallic, if nurturant, male. Both *Deronda* and *Mirth* dispense with this cover story. Resisting the Oedipal plot, their heroines are returned to its pre-Oedipal determinants. As a means of articulating a utopian demand, this return places *Deronda* and *Mirth* in the position of anticipating the *écriture féminine* of the 1970s and early 1980s, which resists phallogocentrism through the creation of a utopian discourse, one that expresses a multivocal, mother-infant-self eroticism.

Allusions to the Persephone myth attend Gwendolyn's reunion with her mother after Grandcourt's death. Grandcourt, who jealously kept Gwendolyn from her mother, is, of course, playing Pluto's role. The trust Gwendolyn has in him is felt, by Deronda, as "the retreating cry of a creature snatched and carried out of his reach by swift horsemen or swifter waves" (683). Echoing *Paradise Lost*, the narrator mentions "the flowery vale of Enna" (824); returning, in her mind, to Offendene, Gwendolyn looks back on the "lure" she followed "through a long Satanic masquerade" (831); while on the journey home, she "sat by like one who had visited the spirit-world and was full to the lips of an unutterable experience" (832). Persephone's ritual return is relevant to *The Winter's Tale*, as well, where Perdita comes back in time to be reunited with her resurrected mother, Hermione. In *Deronda*, Gwendolyn is both returning daughter and awakening Hermione. Toward the end of Book VII and, again, in the final crisis of Book VIII, Gwendolyn is explicitly likened to a "statue," as much earlier she had been when hysteria interrupted her *tableau vivant*, preventing her from enacting Hermione's awakening ("She looked like a statue into which a soul of Fear had entered") (745, 876, 91). Once Deronda has actually abandoned her, Gwendolyn's mother comes upon her "sitting motionless." Responding to her, however, Gwendolyn cries, repeatedly, "Yes mamma. But don't be afraid. I am going to live" (879). This is pretty far from the miraculous coming-to-life dramatized in *The Winter's Tale*. But the note of desperation, the need, repeatedly, to reaffirm her will to live is appropriate to the sadly future-oriented "faith" (explicitly required in *The Winter's Tale*) Gwendolyn's mentor expresses in her before he leaves.

Not permitted even a symbolically ambiguous rebirth, Lily's pre-Oedipal romance occurs solely in the realm of fantasy. As Lily drifts off under the influence of the fatal chloral, she imagines that she cradles Nettle Struther's baby in her arm. This puts her, with Gwendolyn, in the place of the mother, but the impoverished, painfully isolated Lily is clearly also the infant returning to seek reassurance, comfort, and warmth. This scene of baby-bound pleasure expresses a sense of lost possibilities but also of unmet needs so powerful they insist on imaginary fulfillment. Significantly, Lily doesn't merely dream she has the baby at her side: she actually experiences its soft, bodily presence. In her very last moments, a panicky sense of abandonment – "a dark flash of loneliness and terror" – is succeeded by a richly sensuous recovery of the lost child: "She started up again, cold and trembling with the shock: for a moment she seemed to have lost her hold of the child. But no – she was mistaken – the tender pressure of its body was still close to hers: the recovered warmth flowed through her once more, she yielded to it, sank into it, and slept" (II, 13, 251).

In providing Lily with a phantom female child, Wharton rewrites one of Mary Wilkins Freeman's more disturbing supernatural tales, "The Lost Child," published in 1903, just two years before *Mirth*. "The Lost Child" tells of hauntings by a girl ghost whose flesh-and-blood counterpart died of starvation when her mother locked her up in their house before running off with her lover. Wharton, herself a writer of supernatural fiction who suffered maternal neglect, would, I imagine, have been strongly engaged by this tale. One of the women being haunted, Mrs. Bird, a generous, loving woman who has had no children of her own, takes pity on the little spirit and tries to befriend it. One cold winter morning she is seen walking outside with the child, who is holding onto her hand, "nestling close to her as if she had found her own mother." As it turns out, Mrs. Bird has just died; she is discovered lying in her bed with a dreamy smile on her face and an outstretched hand. Here, as in *Mirth*, death arrives with the satisfaction of maternal longings and reunion with a substitute, unreal child. In Freeman's story the lost child, too, is fulfilled. Earlier, however, during her hauntings, she was able to say, repeatedly, only one thing: the simple, plaintive, "I can't find my mother."[33] We're never told what the word is that would make things clear between Lily and Selden. "*Beyond!*" is one possibility, but, given this context, might another be the word that all men know in *Ulysses*? Is it important that the word comes to Lily as she lies at peace with the sleeping child? Though the word remains unspoken, it is clear that, having been abandoned by her mentor, Lily's resistance, like Gwendolyn's, has finally been overcome.[34]

NOTES

1. Samuel Richardson, *Sir Charles Grandison*, ed. Jocelyn Harris (Oxford: Oxford University Press, 1986), vol. VII, 436. All subsequent references to *Grandison* will be to this edition, by volume number and page number.

2. Jane Austen, *Sense and Sensibility*, ed. R. W. Chapman (Oxford: Oxford University Press, 1933), 331. Subsequent parenthetical references to *Sensibility* will be to this edition.

3. Not untypical is Q. D. Leavis's comment on Wharton: "Her admiration of Henry James's work, later her great intimacy with him, provided her with a springboard from which to take off as an artist," in "Henry James's Heiress: The Importance of Edith Wharton," *Scrutiny* (Dec. 1938), rpt. *Edith Wharton*, ed. Irving Howe (Englewood Cliffs, N.J.: Prentice-Hall, 1962), 73–88. The fear that to detect any "influence" by James would be to celebrate Wharton's "discipleship" is discussed by Cushing Strout, "Complementary Portraits:

James's Lady and Wharton's Age," *Hudson Review* 36 (1982): 405–415.

4. Edith Wharton, *The Writing of Fiction* (New York: Charles Scribner's Sons, 1925), 3–29.

5. For an informative discussion of these interrelations, see Constance Rooke, "Beauty in Distress: *Daniel Deronda* and *The House of Mirth*," *Women and Literature* 4 (1976): 28–39.

6. Janice Radway, *Reading the Romance: Women, Patriarchy, and Popular Literature* (Chapel Hill: University of North Carolina Press, 1984), 46–85.

7. Gillian Beer, "Voice and Vengeance: The Poems and *Daniel Deronda*," in her *George Eliot* (Brighton: Harvester Press, 1986), 216, 217.

8. George Eliot, *Daniel Deronda* (Harmondsworth: Penguin, 1967), 222. All further parenthetical references to *Deronda* will be to this edition.

9. Henry James, *"Daniel Deronda*: A Conversation," *Atlantic Monthly* (Dec. 1876): xxxviii, 684–694; rpt. *George Eliot: The Critical Heritage*, ed. David Carroll (London: Routledge and Kegan Paul, 1971), 420.

10. Judith L. Herman and Helen B. Lewis, "Anger in the Mother-Daughter Relationship," in *The Psychology of Today's Woman: New Psychoanalytic Visions*, ed. T. Bernay and D. W. Cantor (Hillside, N.J.: Lawrence Erlbaum, 1986), 139–163.

11. Jessica Benjamin, "Woman's Desire," *The Bonds of Love* (New York: Pantheon, 1988), 85–132.

12. Henry James, *The Portrait of a Lady*, ed. Robert D. Bamberg (New York: Norton, 1975), 84.

13. Jane Austen, *Emma*, ed. R. W. Chapman (Oxford: Oxford University Press, 1944), 86, 269; all subsequent references to *Emma* will be to this edition.

14. See, for example, Sandra Bartky, "Narcissism, Femininity and Alienation," in her *Femininity and Domination: Studies in the Phenomenology of Oppression* (New York: Routledge, 1990), 33–44. In her highly influential " 'The Blank Page' and the Issues of Female Creativity," Susan Gubar includes *Deronda*, *Portrait*, and *Mirth* in her wide-ranging discussion of aestheticization, infantalization, and narcissism as features of women's oppression under patriarchy, *Critical Enquiry* 8 (1982): 243–263.

15. Mary Wollstonecraft, *A Vindication of the Rights of Woman*, ed. Miriam Kramnick (Harmondsworth: Penguin, 1985), 223. All subsequent references to *Vindication* will be to this edition. This passage serves as opening epigraph to Cora Kaplan's brilliant "Wild Nights:

Pleasure/Sexuality/Feminism," in her *Sea Changes: Culture and Feminism* (London: Verso, 1986), 31.

16. Kaplan, "Wild Nights," 37.

17. Janet Todd discusses Sir Charles's exemplary status in *Sensibility: An Introduction* (London: Methuen, 1986), 69–77.

18. Wharton, *Writing of Fiction*, 110.

19. Carole Pateman, *The Sexual Contract* (Stanford: Stanford University Press, 1988), 116–153.

20. "Her knowledge of Richardson's works was such as no one is likely again to acquire. . . . Every circumstance narrated in Sir Charles Grandison, all that was ever said or done in the cedar parlour, was familiar to her; and the wedding days of Lady L. and Lady G. were as well remembered as if they had been living friends." James E. Austen-Leigh, *Memoir of Jane Austen*, ed. R. W. Chapman (Oxford: Clarendon Press, 1926), 89.

21. Juliet McMaster discusses the inseparability for Austen of pedagogy and genuine romantic passion in "Love and Pedagogy," in her *Jane Austen on Love* (Victoria: University of Victoria English Literary Studies, 1978), 43–65.

22. See *The George Eliot Letters*, vol. II, ed. Gordon S. Haight (New Haven: Yale University Press, 1954): "Delicious walk; sat on Castle hill and M. read *Emma* aloud,"G. H. Lewes Journal, [11]–18 May 1857, 327, 328; and vol. VI (1955), 171.

23. "I had no idea that Richardson was worth so much. I have had more pleasure from him than from all the Swedish novels together. The morality is perfect – there is nothing for the new lights to correct." George Eliot to Sara S. Hennell, 13 October [1847], *Letters*, vol. I (1954), 240. See also, "Like Sir Charles Grandison? I should be sorry to be the heathen that did not like that book," vol. II, 65; and vol. VI (1955), 320.

24. Jacqueline Rose relates the "hysterisation" of women to anxieties about social order and cohesion in England during the second half of the nineteenth century, anxieties that were articulated by various medical, social, and political discourses. Eliot, she argues, participates in this movement by making Gwendolyn, from the very opening scene of the novel, "the privileged object of investigation and control." "George Eliot and the Spectacle of the Woman," in her *Sexuality in the Field of Vision* (London: Verso, 1986), 113.

25. D. R. Carroll explores interrelations between the two central, contrasting visions in "The Unity of 'Daniel Deronda,'" *Essays in Criticism* 9 (1959): 369–380.

26. See Mariana Valverde's discussion of medical and political discourses of social regulation in "The Love of Finery: Fashion and the Fallen Woman in Nineteenth-Century Social Discourse," *Victorian Studies* 32 (1989): 169–188.

27. Wharton, *The Writing of Fiction*, 63, 64.

28. For a superb discussion of the multifold dynamics of the exchange system and of "the commodification of social intercourse" in *Mirth*, see Wai-Chee Dimock, "Debasing Exchange: Edith Wharton's *The House of Mirth*," in *Edith Wharton*, ed. Harold Bloom (New York: Chelsea House, 1986), 128–137.

29. For an excellent discussion of *Deronda*'s constitution of the *reader* as spectator in this scene, see Rose, "George Eliot and the Spectacle of the Woman," 116–122.

30. Dimock's discussion of this passage sees it as expressing "a quintessentially aristocratic ideal" – "Debasing Exchange," 136.

31. James, *The Portrait of a Lady*, 478.

32. Catherine Gallagher argues that usury, prostitution, and art are complexly interrelated in Eliot's later works, in "George Eliot and *Daniel Deronda*: The Prostitute and the Jewish Question," *Sex, Politics, and Science in the Nineteenth-Century Novel: Selected Papers from the English Institute, 1983–84*, ed. Ruth Bernard Yeazell (Baltimore: Johns Hopkins University Press, 1986), 39–62.

33. I am grateful to Catherine Lundy for introducing me to this story.

34. Written in 1987, this essay has undergone only the most minor revisions; I've not made any attempt to bring it up to date. At the time of writing, questions about the specificity of an Anglo-American female literary tradition were uppermost in my mind, as I had for several years been teaching an English course in Major Women Writers. Were I to revise the essay, I would want to develop the notion that in this tradition both male mentorship and female resistance are implicitly racialized. Two essays I've published since may be of interest to some readers: "Wanting Protection: 'Fair Ladies', Sensibility and Romance," in *Mary Woolstonecraft and 200 Years of Feminisms*, ed. Eileen Yeo (London: Rivers Oram Press, 1997), 61–85, and "Romance in the Forbidden Zone," in *Re-Imagining Women: Representations of Women in Culture*, ed. Shirley Neuman and Glennis Stephenson (Toronto: University of Toronto Press, 1993), 160–181.

4

Beyond Her Self

THOMAS LOEBEL

In interpreting Miss Bart's state of mind, so many alternative readings were possible. (II, 3, 165)

The teeth of *The House of Mirth* are the ways in which the upper-class social system in New York at the turn of the century is laid bare for critical judgment. The commodification of persons, the sex/gender economy, the radical capitalism of human relations presented by the text and amplified by subsequent readers remain as reminders of the power of materialism in its attempt to render society commensurable and exchangeable all the way to its most constituent parts, the human in the person and sociality in society. However, heightened awareness of our own production and perpetuation of this economy does not seem to have altered our behavior terribly much for the better. One could argue that we have rather complexified the processes completely out of hand, achieving for the system a kind of ubiquity that has an inuring effect on consciousness. When coercive agents and personal complicity get multiplied at every point, the task of critique and repair looms too monumental to mount. *The House of Mirth* may grab our interest, but only as part of a genealogical discovery of the earlier, simpler system and its relation to our own. It wants us to identify with its version of a captivity narrative, but we may well be past the point at which this text can really scare us about what the commodification of human relations produces.

Yet *The House of Mirth* is still a profoundly disturbing novel, less because of the discovery of what society can do than because of what it presents as the process of *self*-discovery that Lily under-

107

goes in response to the effects of society. For this is, I would argue, centrally a novel of self-discovery. The economic market of society continues its circulation unchanged from the beginning to the end of the novel. What alters is Lily Bart. The sublimity of reading *The House of Mirth*, however, is that change for the good (Lily's resistance to commodification and exchange) seems to result in something awful, her death. Why? Why when she is such a skilled player in the market does Lily Bart begin to act in ways other than those that would guarantee her success? If she has come to realize the depravity of the social system, why does she not learn from Lawrence Selden and find her own way into the "republic of the spirit"? If she has come to realize that moral choices and ethical behavior have an immeasurable and hence other worth than that constructed by the social system, why does she overdose on chloral? My response to these questions is that none of them can be answered in any definitive and logical way when the thrust of this text is to chart a radical destabilization of Lily's identity as she moves beyond the system in which she would be readable. The answers would come from "beyond," which is first beyond the language and the sense of the question.

If the system is, broadly speaking, one of human commodification, then its particular application is the stock market social economy of New York's nouveau riche society. The move in this text beyond comes in two stages: first, beyond the social economy; then beyond even the economy's governing system, the construction of identities that can be commodified and thus circulated. While Lily Bart recognizes the socioeconomic system of identity construction, the ability to make that recognition presumes at least a cognitive move outside the realm that always seeks to dissemble its control of agency and cognition. To recognize the social economy as an application of the system is coterminous with the understanding that identity is not equal to being, but rather a cognitive enclosure within it, a way of making sense of being. Being is more and other than identity, more than this dominant way of making sense. Yet in recognizing the displacement of identity, one must respond to the strangeness of being and dis-cover oneself, which does not secure identity and its ontological boundaries but rather enables identity to go beyond its self. An encounter with the strangeness of being makes no sense, at least no sense as constructed by the terms of the social economy, and no sense of identity. Further, I would argue that according to the rhetoric and plot of this novel, an encounter with the strangeness of being enables passage beyond sense entirely, beyond even a cognitive reconstruction of being as a new identity. For to respond in such an encounter is not to operate within an economy of sense and cognition. The very ways in which sense is made as identity are precisely those which are persecuted by the encounter with being other than as identity, with the stranger of being. Yet, as identity is troubled by being, so being in turn finds itself persecuted by its own possibility. If the strangeness of being first debits the profits of identity, then in a discovery that goes further beyond, the entire economy of cognition is ultimately wiped off the slate. One is left a stranger in being, stripped of place, without securities, discovered if not found.

Identity may well be a social construction always deconstructing within response to the strangerliness of being, but the very boundaries of thinking being, ontology and ontic discourse, deconstruct as thought ventures beyond to what enabled its own possibility, in much the same way that being enables and renders impossible stable and singular identity itself. Being itself is a certain impossibility in the sense that there is no self-identicality to being. It comes to be in relation to an other, prior to itself, to which being constructs itself to be in response. This other is a stranger more strange than the strangerliness of being, other than the human of being, yet it is in relation to the stranger that everything we call human is made manifest. The trace of this alterity is the essentiality of the human in being as ontology constructs it, the core of the self as we call it, the soul. The process of self-discovery both *within* and *of* being dis-covers the non-self-identity of being, that being is a being-for-the-other, here an otherwise than being itself.

According to these terms, *The House of Mirth* can be read as a narrative of a woman who doesn't really want what she has been brought up to want, who can't perform the sorts of transactions that deal unethically with other persons, even though these motivate the social relations in this society; who is, therefore, a misfit, without a place, who cannot live alone and therefore dies. Such a reading, however, misses the opportunity to think the theoretical possibilities for an ethics of self-discovery generated by Wharton's text. Both within and beyond its narration, what the text performs is the process of dis-covering the complex relations of identity, being and beyond, of dis-covering the being of the self and the being-for of being. The enduring agony of this performance is that dis-covering the self is an impossibility within being. In order to address the soul of "who I am," one moves beyond being, articulating otherwise. Lily Bart does dis-cover herself, but removing the cover occurs as a movement beyond being, beyond cognition and consciousness, beyond language. What *The House of Mirth* gives us is an articulation of the self as passage, as response to the alterity of the soul, taking it beyond being.

> She was so evidently the victim of the civilization which had produced her. (I, 1, 8).

Identity is thought carefully in this text, because there are no characters who are so fully socially constructed that they do not recognize that being, with all of its possibilities, exceeds the identity of the subject. All seem to know that identity is a *way* of being, constructed within the terms and limitations set by the social system. As with money in an exchange economy, identity is the currency of the system of being. Either to be without it, or to assume that it is everything, is to be lost. Lily suggests, for instance, that "the only way not to think about money is to have a great deal of it" (I, 6, 56), whereas Selden counters:

> . . . you might as well say that the only way not to think about air is to have enough to breathe. That is true enough in a sense; but your lungs are thinking about the air, if you are not. And so it is with your rich people – they may not be thinking of money, but they're breathing it all the while; take them into another element and see how they squirm and gasp! (I, 6, 56).

The major players in this text are entirely conscious of identity's gilded cage. Even those who seem most constructed – Mrs. Peniston, for example, who rarely gives glimpses that she might be otherwise than she is – still manifest behavior readable as a marker of this knowledge. Mrs. Peniston's house becomes a figure for her sense of self, her enclosure of identity, whose constituent parts are carefully arranged, polished, and accounted for annually. "She 'went through' the linen and blankets in the precise spirit of the penitent exploring the inner folds of conscience" (I, 9, 78). Yet placed within this identity, "her mind resembled one of those little mirrors which her Dutch ancestors were accustomed to affix to their upper windows, so that from the depths of an impenetrable domesticity they might see what was happening in the street" (I, 3, 32). Those of Lily's set fully recognize that conduct and the measured representations of identity project not *who* they are but *what* they are, not all of their being but its most visible edifice. People are victims of this construction not only when they are not at home in this house, but also when they cannot get out. Or worse, they are victims when they are ambivalent about venturing forth, dis-covering, de-constructing the edifice of identity within being, as is the case with Lily. If the republic of the spirit is meant to signify "personal freedom . . . from everything" (I, 6, 55), its negative libertarian definition necessitates a pulling apart and removal of the boundary between identity construction and the multiplicity of being. That this is a republic that "one has to find the way to one's self" (I, 6, 55) indicates not only that this is a project motivated by self-will, but also, as Wharton's choice of phrase suggests, that to find the way to the republic is to find "one's self," elsewhere than in the socially constructed confines of identity.

As a way of acting within being, identity is a certain vocation. It is purposive, a construction of skills meant to (trans)form the material of the self into a successful player following a reason for being. "Isn't marriage your vocation? Isn't it what you're all brought up for?" Selden asks (I, 1, 10). Women are engendered for marriage, and the whole construction of gendered identity is about teaching women how to shape and deploy their physical assets for attraction and their public personae for promoting men, while shoring up the blinders of consciousness necessary for believing that they are powerfully acting out self-directed behavior. The rhetoric describing Lily speaks on the one hand of her being "produced," saying that "she must have cost a great deal to make" (I, 1, 7), yet on the other it describes the tasks of her vocation in terms of hunting, her "method of attack (I, 3, 17), the men as "prey" (17), thought as powerless against her skillfully deployed beauty. What brings the two discourses together is that of the commodity, with the word "asset" standing on the threshold between social construction and seemingly self-directed power. For it can be said that the "vocation" of the commodity is to be bought, and everything about the look of the thing and what it does for the consumer is granted a *power* of attraction. While capitalist economic systems market acquisition and the ability to purchase as a means of power, there is power afforded to the commodity as well, in terms of a variety of discourses of attraction: rarity, beauty, reliability, and so forth. Wharton's text of a capitalistic social system maps the power dynamics onto the gendered identity of the different sexes, inscribing marriage as the fundamental purchase transaction motivating the system. Marriage is not the raison d'être of existence, but it is a motivating reason by and for which gendered identity is constructed. Goods produced that can't be sold, unmarriageable women and men without means, are remaindered into the bargain bin and eventually excluded from the system altogether. They are discontinued.

Unlike inanimate objects, few human commodities go quietly or happily. Even when circulating in an economy of arbitrary values with a tremendously forceful system of construction, the trace of human worth that remains in the commodification of persons introduces what we might call ontological trouble into a system that wishes to set value according to the economy of exchange. Pork bellies don't have ontological crises when their value plummets against their will. Obviously, pork bellies don't have "will." They have existence, but no soul; fluctuating value, but not a trace of eternal worth as such. Fundamentally they have no self, no possibility of being a subject. Human commodities possess the possibility of selfhood in the interstices between their objective existence as commodities in circulation and their being as subjects – between, one might say, two ontological discourses, as object (of) and subject (to). Dis-covering the self is a process that takes place between these two. The trace of the human in being persecutes the commodified object of identity, and response to the trace of the human (or what I am calling the soul) is the very process of dis-covering the full ontological self, a coming into being of the self.

There is an ethics of self-discovery, then, in that as persecuted by being, identity and self-identicality are called into question so radically by this other as to enable their deconstruction.[1] The other (in) being of the self faces identity, persecuting its cognitive construction as a reason for being. In the mute language of trauma, the human faces the commodity demanding response. This process is no simple one. It always runs the risk of a certain failure, whereby the other (in) being is conceptualized as just another part of my self, some alternative "me," and thus imperialistically brought within identity's boundaries. Lily wrestles with this possibility after the jarring event on the Sabrina. "She felt that she had at last arrived at an understanding with herself: had made a pact with her rebellious impulses, and achieved a uniform system of self-government, under which all vagrant tendencies were either held captive or forced into the service of the state" (II, 1, 150). As the text suggests, reconstructing identity imperialistically is a project of understanding, of making sense of being, of generating new reasons for being, all articulated within a rhetoric of capture and force. Lily achieves a certain republic of the spirit as a system of self-government, ironizing Selden's version. Rather than approaching the stranger self of being, letting it be, her understanding pulls the stranger self into a *uni*form system, attempting to maintain at all costs its self-identi(cali)ty.

It might be odd to suggest that ethical self-discovery must not involve understanding, or understanding that conscripts the difference of the other in being to an identity of sameness. But the text goes further to implicate not only understanding, but also thinking itself. During the important moment of ontological trouble concerning the republic of the spirit, the text flags that "there were in her at the moment two beings" (I, 6, 52), and these two appear after the crisis with Trenor, when Lily's commodified identity would have had her submit to rape. Yet here is distinctly added, "I can't think – I can't think, she moaned. . . . She seemed a stranger to herself, or rather there were two selves in her, the one she had always known, and a new abhorrent being to which it found itself chained" (I, 13, 117). Both scenes are important in marking Lily's trajectory out of high society, and both mark the stranger within. What is remarkable here is that the relation between the one self and the other is not communicated by cognition, nor even so much by its lack, but by its inability. One can't think when in proximity to the stranger within. As the text continues, this space of separation is amplified by a divide in temporality. "There was a great gulf fixed between today and yesterday" (I, 13, 117), as great as that between the one and the other of the self, even as the two are inextricably "chained." Both thematically and philosophically, the gap registers the discontinuities fundamental to thinking being, and the questioning of thought within being. As she questions who she is, the terms mark a distinctly strange relation of proximity and distance, radical space and enclosure, time and its breach. If self-discovery is the project of coming to terms with one's strangerliness in time, then what Wharton's rhetoric suggests is that its possibility within ontology is constituted by structures unable to be made manifest within the self's intelligibility – not a cognitive relation between one and another, but its inability within the time of ontology. This is not to say that the relation does not happen or take place. It does, but in an "other time," which I mean in two senses.

First, self-discovery begins in the continuous temporal flow of the here and now, only to discover radical discontinuity – not just a broken time, but rather an otherwise than time. All of its self-referential questioning (which is, by extension, ontic discourse as such) cannot think itself *through* this gulf, this other-relation of time, but only *to* it. Second, if self-discovery is to be true, it must be true to the other prior to the self. Faced with the other (in) being, on the brink of an otherwise than time, self-discovery must dis-cover itself, but as a radical opening to that which it does not and cannot understand. Dis-covering is not finding oneself. The process is not self-referential by which everything is understood, made safe, and thus re-covered. Rather, dis-covering the self, true to the other, pushes itself to the absolute limit, face to face in confrontation with the manifestation of alterity. Not to do so is to thwart the project of self *dis*-covery with *re*-covery. Dis-covery must be an ethical relation to the other self, to take place on the other's terms and the other's time, both of which are not understandable to the identitarian self. One must journey beyond sense, beyond time and the thought of time as continuous with presence, to an unthinkable time that maintains all the priority of the ethical relation while providing the truth of being. This would be to enter a space of time that does not exist as such, but is dead time, a breach of time, the time of the other, and otherwise than temporality as we think it. According to John Llewelyn, following Emmanuel Levinas, "absolute alterity requires that this continuity be interrupted by dead time, *temps mort.*"[2] "There must be a rupture of this continuity, and continuation across this rupture," such as the chain across the gap of space and time suggests in *The House of Mirth*.[3] For these reasons is the "Beyond!" of Lily Bart readable as indicating an elsewhere that is an otherwise. In keeping with the double gestures of words in this text, ones ontological that trace the metaphysical, "*Beyond!*" suggests that Lily's death at the end of the novel is a figure for the dead time of self-discovery.

Ultimately, then, Lily's problem and the issues in this text are more radical than the thematics of difference in society. At significant moments, when Lily's awareness of her alterity within is aligned with how she registers to her peers as different, the text speaks of unbridgeable gaps, spaces in time, which are not *in* the flow of time, but mark a beyond of it, indicating the limit of ontology. The gaps of time and space in being point to what an ontic discourse of anxiety and lack of understanding can trace within its thematizations, but which they cannot articulate to presence. "*Beyond!*" then, closes and is enclosed within what can be said, yet it also makes an impression of that which is otherwise than all that is here and now, present to, and presented by the self.

The space and time in which Lily seeks to find herself is traced in the fundamental scene of the novel, that of the *tableaux vivants*.

Tableaux vivants depend for their effect not only on the happy disposal of lights and the delusive interposition of layers of gauze, but on a corresponding adjustment of the mental vision. To unfurnished minds they remain, in spite of every enhancement of art, only a superior kind of wax-works; but to the responsive fancy they may give magic glimpses of the boundary world between fact and imagination. (I, 12, 105)

Lily's mind is furnished with the corresponding adjustment of the mental vision, which is synonymous, as the text suggests, with being responsive. The kind of "response" Lily makes, however, is to the stranger within. This is to say that her sense moves toward the other of sense, and even beyond, into the otherwise than sense in which the soul of being takes its priority. This movement is pertinent to the *tableaux vivants*, because these performances are all about a relation of the self to another, over the gulf of a certain death and unbridgeable space, and yet the relation is mutually revelatory. The everyday subjectivity of the person "dies" into a figure from a canvas, bringing it to life. At the same time, and through the dying of the subjectivity of the self, the figure from the picture brings out "the real Lily Bart, divested of the trivialities of her little world, and catching for a moment a note of that eternal harmony" (I, 12, 106).[4] Such harmony, I would translate, is generated by the soul of the self, caught for a moment of dead time, able to flicker within existence only (if not able to come to be) by way of the confluence of the one losing her self in the other as response.[5]

What interests me is this moment of the passage into dead time that is prior to the conscious registration of what is being seen as intelligible. The moment that Selden and Gerty Farish see and know the real Lily Bart in the *tableau* may well be real, to employ Wharton's term, but it is already too late to be true. In constructing the thematic of the real Lily Bart and then registering it as seen, the mind performs a cognitive operation that seems instantaneous and immediate. What we get *is* the moment, which is the trace-effect of an attempt to bridge the gulf, as well as an attempt to translate the truth of the other into the moment. What results is the construction of the real (in the) time of the one. However, "the truth correlative to being – in which the subject, a pure welcome reserved for the nudity of disclosed being, effaces itself *before* that which manifests itself, and in which effort, inventiveness, and genius are all just means, ways, and detours by which being is dis-covered, by which its phases come together and its structures are secured – remains, within the thought that issued from Greece, the foundation of every notion of truth."[6] The move to make the thematization of the truth of being manifest within intelligibility, to secure it within the structure of what we call the self, is a reaction to the "hesitation, a time, a certain risk, good or bad fortune" constitutive of the always only about to come to be of the truth of the human.[7] Accepting alterity on its own terms and time is otherwise even than "letting it be," for one does not even assume the power relation of "letting." Perhaps fitting in Wharton's context of economy and circulation is to approach this relation not as exchange but as gift, a giving over of the self in a certain expenditure without return, a circumvention of the imperialism of intelligibility.[8]

Both Gerty and Selden function entirely within the stock market economy of this text at this moment, in the sense that neither faces pure risk and gives all.[9] The question is whether one can do otherwise when the structure of intelligibility as it comes down through Western philosophy is capitalistically imperialist itself. How is it possible not to have the real overtake the true within intelligibility and its thematizations? The word "soul," for instance, is a name standing in for the absolute alterity of the human that cannot but be lost in language. One can say that in seeing the real Lily Bart, Gerty and Selden have caught a glimpse of her soul, but this discourse itself is an attempt to *trans*-scribe what cannot be rendered in its own terms. The terms of cognition *take it over.* The soul, as we say, is not really existent but transscendent. It can't be found. It figures the truth of being with a word that designates uncognizable immateriality. Yet what I find interesting in Wharton's structure of the *tableau vivant* is the attempt, within the possibilities afforded by narrative description, to trace the sort of space one finds within a shadow, a space in which the nudity of being is itself being traced within objective intelligibility.

If *tableaux vivants* are threshold structures dependent upon the blurring of the boundaries between art and life, and between what is seen and what is made intelligible, then the choice of Reynold's portrait of Mrs. Lloyd particularly carries the threshold structure toward the thematics of nudity, alterity, and being-for-the-other. The "pale draperies" of the dress enable the shadowy appearance of "the female outline" (I, 12, 107), which in turn is dis-closed as "the touch of poetry in her beauty" (I, 12, 106). Full of suggestion, then, is the constellated connection of traces and figures, outline and poetry. There is the possibility within representation – particularly one so double as that of a *tableau vivant* – for the figural to trace the otherwise than intelligible, in such a way as to efface the alterity of the soul as it will by definition, but at the same time and within the coming to be within time to efface the totality of appearance within intelligibility. In figuring the other, allegorized by the act of Lily's modeling, what is carried over may exceed what is intelligible to consciousness. There may be a trace of alterity, manifested but unthematizable. While the thematic of the real Lily Bart is not equal to the truth of her held by the other, it may trace the truth. This claim suggests that at the same time that it signifies within ontology, language signifies otherwise, (in) the time of the other, the dead time in which alterity makes its approach as about to come to be.

The ability for language to signify so doubly and differently would have to be thought beyond the limit of any conscious control of language's use. The other dis-closes language, which is traceable in language, opening up the possibility of the self's conscious attempt to respond and address, but also to know not what it does. One cannot properly confess this stranger strangerliness in being, because it is unintelligible as shock, capture, being held in the face of alterity, not of the known self but of the human in being signifying its priority in and of an other time. This is alterity showing its face, but such a face as cannot be made manifest within intelligibility on its own terms. When it is made manifest, it signifies in the language of the self, but this mode of signification is not wholly known to the self, even while it might be entirely recognizable.

According to Emmanuel Levinas, when the face of the other sets forth its signifyingness to ontology, this ethical saying will be taken to signify as said, a signification of and for intelligibility, but "the plot of the saying that is absorbed in the said is not exhausted in this manifestation. It imprints its trace on the thematization itself, which hesitates between, on the one hand, structuration, order of a configuration of entities . . . and on the other hand, the order of non-nominalized apophansis of the other, in which the said remains a *proposition*, a proposition made to a neighbor, 'a signifyingness dealt' (*significance baililée*) to the other."[10] "One must show in saying, qua approach, the very deposing or desituating of the subject, which nonetheless remains an irreplaceable uniqueness, and is thus the subjectivity of the subject."[11] Manifesting the figural within thematization can give more than intelligibility can take, as a certain surplus that cannot be appropriated and rendered into sense. Yet sensation, as prior to sense, responds to this unheard call, tracing within the figural the about-to-come-to-be, the priority, of subjectivity. The scene of the *tableaux vivants* is certainly one in which the audience for the *tableaux* and the reader are reacting to the outline, the traced body, the certain dis-closing taking place, very much in terms of the real Lily Bart; yet within that thematic we are witness to the dis-covery of Lily Bart herself, in which the nudity of her alterity is traced in the difference of representation as (her) absolute self. What corroborates this witnessing are the actions of the figure in the scene, which is to say here, what Lily/Mrs. Lloyd is doing. She is caught inscribing her initials on a tree, in love with an other. If the other for Mrs. Lloyd is external to her as another person, then Lily's enacting of this scene figures its significance in ways more appropriate to her situation. The other is not external, and this reading turns on the other sense of the "initial." Lily marks her initial self, the other that has priority for the self, the soul. As I have suggested, "The soul is the other within me."[12] There is no other for Lily except that which is for the self.

The traditional and popular conception of selfhood derives from the Cartesian subject, in the sense that not only does thought constitutively prove the existence of being, but the activity of thinking also motivates the subject along the project of selfhood, which will always involve a relation with thinking. "Cogito ergo sum," or "I am thinking, therefore I exist."[13] The cogito provides the most potent thematic of subjectivity within being, such that the whole subsequent project of self-development and discovery is based upon the "I" thinking, trying to understand its relation within being. The result is a very subject-centered self, a self-controlled and hegemonic self, even when troubled and in quest of itself. There is nothing within the cogito that would give priority to self-development involving a subject not functioning within a relation to thought and control, or a subject responding to an other in such a way as to take place prior to the subject's own appropriative act of cognition.[14] One of the things *The House of Mirth* is telling us is that the most important moments of self-discovery occur when the subject finds itself outside of the economy of appropriation and exchange – not simply off the market, but beyond it, when and where the subject can't think itself, because it is transfixed by an alterity within to which it must respond, yet toward which it cannot think. Lily Bart's trajectory in the novel is one that moves from the commodity to the human, from the economic to the moral. This direction suggests a potential for thinking "humanistically" in a theologico-philosophical mode as a way of approaching the self in discovery of Wharton's text.

Throughout, I have been using the term "soul" as a marker of the alterity to which the identitarian subject must respond in the impossible project of self dis-covery. The claim, then, is that a subject is not a self until it sets forth from the construction of identity initiated as response to this alterity, marked as the limit of being. The identitarian subject is a purposive construction, an enclosure for safety, an individual with the other outside of itself, with both set in an economy of relations of appropriation. As the dis-covery of the self is a movement in defiance of identity and appropriation within an approach antithetical to the circulating economy of exchange, it is giving as giving over to the other (in) being that does not return to the subject. Such a response does not expand knowledge, nor operate as know-how. It is unconditional as beyond conditionality, and the conditions of space and time within ontology. Because of this process, I am marking the alterity of being as the soul, hoping to work with the traditional understanding of the soul as neither thing nor place, but as given purely as the human in the nighest proximity to being. To make this articulation initially is to admit that the dis-covered self, the self ethically responding to the soul, is *existent* within ontology. There is no getting outside of this discourse for the purposes of articulation. Indeed, the project of self dis-covery is still one cast in relation to thought, though I would argue that it is not one circulating within an economy of comprehension. Yet as a marker of alterity, a figure of the difference of self and other to the self, "soul" attempts a performance that traces the priority of the human, or what constitutes the absolute fullness of the human always persecuting being. In a Levinasian sense, soul is a "Saying of a Said that the Said dissimulates; but a dissimulation that the saying always seeks to unsay (*dédire*) – which is its ultimate veracity."[15]

To think the soul theologico-philosophically adapts a short passage on the coming to be of the self in Franz Rosenzweig's *Star of Redemption*.[16] Here Rosenzweig details that the subject comes to be a self when it gains its soul. This does not take place in the moment of creation but only after the subject takes hold of its freedom, which is a difficult one indeed. For as human, our freedom is finite, yet we demand that it be unconditional as well. Unconditionality outlines the image of God in which we are made. The demand for unconditionality is, according to Rosenzweig, the moment in which humanity becomes *self-conscious*, defying finitude with unconditionality. Defiance, then, constitutes the soul of humanity, and it is the approach of the soul and the response of the human to it in which the self as such comes to be.

My deployment of this narrative for *The House of Mirth* locates itself first within the thematic of a very odd defiance of the subject within the project of self-discovery, yet the adaptation is to think defiance more radically given the rhetoric of this novel. While I would agree that the self comes to be in relation to the soul, I would offer up "soul" as a signifier for that which is entirely other for the subject trying to dis-cover its self. For as the subject begins to dis-cover its (other) self, the soul makes its approach as an alterity demanding response. If there is defiance in relation to the soul, it is first a defiance of cognition, all associated with the unconditionality of will, that is, a will to be other than a product/project of cognition. This is not just to defy thought in the sense of "I will not think," which takes its relay as decision through cognition. This defiance is other than cognition, other than being as thought within cognition.[17] It is response prior to becoming obligated, and any of the moral imperatives of the "ought" in the Kantian sense. Not only is the narrative of Lily Bart that of an ethical self-discovery, but this process moves her entirely beyond the commodifying economy and its rules of appropriation.

To speak of the move from the self-identicality of identity to the other (in) being as an ethical relation to the stranger and now soulful self is to translate into a philosophical discourse the thematics of Wharton's text as it is punctuated by important figural indices. It is more than, though centrally derived from, the idea that Lily Bart becomes increasingly a stranger to society the more she responds to the stranger within. Where the deconstruction of identity as the responsibility of the self is played out in this text is in terms of gender, and it is here that the text does its most forward-looking work. For as Lily comes to be stranger, she is, according to the text, decidedly "queer." What I want to follow through is not the attribution that the queer has much to do with a same-sex orientation of desire, but that it has everything to do with a stranger relation to a gendered identity of the feminine as it is constructed in this economy of exchange. Ultimately, the ethics of self dis-covery is an ethical relation to the queer in any gendered identity, a response to the que(e)ry posed by the relation of gender to being.

Throughout the narrative, and particularly in Book II, Lily moves further and further into the realm of the queer the more socially excluded and unable to think straight she becomes. From what are explicitly figured as "adventures . . . some queer ones!" (II, 1, 152), all the way to embodying the queer, such that Rosedale blurts, "if I married you now I'd queer myself for good and all" (II, 7, 200), we are reminded that Lily has always flirted with the queer, each time within a discourse of separation. Even though Lily has always had a "craving for the external finish of life" (I, 3, 22), pulling the performance of that phrase to its read-ability as a certain "death drive," she has never been able to take herself wholly toward, let alone beyond, the gap between iden-tity and being, while under the guardianship of Mrs. Peniston. As Lord Hubert recounts to Selden, "there used to be an aunt somewhere . . . who was great at bridging over chasms she [Lily] didn't see" (II, 1, 152). But without her guard, Lily can let the one being, her "free spirit" (I, 6, 52) as it is termed, sail beyond, "out again on those dark seas" called "the mounting tide of indebtedness" (I, 7, 62). Here, of course, I'm reading the "other side," so to say, of these phrases, allowing the other and more radical sense of indebtedness to signify the hostage state of being of the one for the other within the self. Those "dark seas" of self-discovery translate Lily to the Emporium of Mrs. Hatch, in which the players "seemed to float together outside the bounds of time and space . . . night and day flowed into one another in a blur of confused and retarded engagements" (II, 9, 214). As opposed to Selden's conclusion to Lily that "you don't know where you are!" (II, 9, 217), "Lily had an odd sense of being behind the social tapestry, on the side where the threads were knotted and the loose ends hung" (II, 9, 215).

This is the realm of the queer, the other side. The tapestry is a figure for the discursive weave constructing the being of self in society, language threaded into the figures of the here and now. And here the queer as the stranger side of language exists. In one sense, one can think the relation between metaphysics and ontol-ogy as the one and the other sides of the tapestry. Language constructs the possibility of speaking both, yet the figures that ontically appear within a certain thematics, indeed all that is made manifest by cognition, have a relation to an other side that is both fundamentally linked/chained to it, but which an ontic discourse cannot fully bring to presence. The trace of what ontol-ogy figures can be thought from the figures of ontology them-selves, but it is not made present in the same place and time. It is always beyond them. Ontology can figure what constitutes its possibility of being, both in, yet anterior to it, only as a narrative of "In the beginning," attempting to thematize beginning as time and priority. In gendered terms, gendered representations and constructions of femininity and masculinity are constituted by queer threads linked over a threshold. The queer is neither the ground of gender construction, nor a backdrop or context, but rather the "other side" of the being of persons, which, under our still current though waning value scheme, is turned to face the wall because it is not neat, its colors wrong, its shaping coarse, according to the hegemonic aesthetic.

To be queer, to find the self of gendered identity in a queer relation to its other and to respond, goes beyond altering the components of gendered identity, or simply changing the way a woman acts. Lily's queer behavior, appearing both to the eyes of society and to her former self, is certainly a manifestation of her internal persecution, but acting differently and shoring up a different and more feminist-seeming identity is not the telos of self dis-covery, nor is it Lily's project at all. I do not mean this as a critique of feminism and the fundamentally necessary work taking place within contemporary identity politics, but it is difficult to see Lily Bart as a feminist protagonist in practical political terms. As she says to Gerty Farish, "I want admiration, I want excitement, I want money – yes, *money!*" (I, 14, 132), and these take their meaning within the social economy of her set. She wants exactly what her socially constructed gendered identity has molded her for, but that very identity cages her with only one way to get such things. Certainly, then, the mental, physical, and material caging of women forms both the tragedy and the ground of the critique in this text. Lily can see out of her cage, but she can't seem to get out. Even though alternative ways of living and acting are presented to her, becoming another *type* of woman is not what Lily achieves, nor is it what this text is about. Rather, the text focuses on the *inability* of identity to become something different. What I am suggesting, however, is that this type of reading is possible and makes sense particularly if one is reading the text only within the terms of an ontic discourse, of needs and desires, perception and understanding, confined within language to constructions within ontology. But if we follow where Lily goes in the language of the queer, to the other side of the tapestry, an other relation to ontology, identity, and gender asserts its priority.

So far I have suggested a number of queer relations: that identity is not equal to being; that the identitarian subject is persecuted by an other (of) being within; that to respond to this other is to begin the ethics of self dis-covery; that ethical response is not a cognitive operation, but a relation otherwise; that the being of the other self speaks figurally or shows its face within ontology and an ontic discourse, but the latter is able to make manifest only the difference of the other. Such a manifestation is sufficient to trouble identity, because difference figurally traces the alterity existent beyond it. The moments of ontological trouble in this text are also moments of gender trouble, in which feminine identity faces the difference of being possible for existence. And herein lies the fundamental philosophical distinction of Wharton's text: whenever the difference of being confronts the identity of femininity, ontological discourse begins to get "gauzy," if not unreadable. I have been suggesting that these moments of an inability to think, or those of perception tracing the gauzy outline of a figure, are ones in which the confrontation of difference within ontology traces an alterity beyond being, beyond the difference of being, and beyond a gendered identity construction. These are, to suggest the connection to Levinas and his rendering of the ethical, moments in which the Said of the soul tries to unsay itself *as if* the alterity beyond ontology could *Say* purely within it.

After the trial with Gus Trenor, when Lily comes to Gerty Farish's for the night – arguably the most important set of scenes in which Lily must confront the relation between her two selves – she figures the shock to identity from this other self in terms of "disfigurement. . . . I seem to myself like that" (I, 14, 131). The figure of disfigurement, within the context of ontic discourse, and relayed through the thematic of identity and its other, performs the figure *as* disfigurement. Dis-figurement is the way in which language tries to unsay itself, which is no translation to the literal as ground, or permanence, or the real. Rather dis-figurement marks the trace of the other's face, otherwise than as figural appearance.

When language takes this turn, and ontological discourse traces an other/wise in a circumlocutionary act, the threshold inscribed between identity and being calls for passage beyond, to an otherwise than being, an otherwise than saying with a priority of pure communication other than in a language manifested for being in consciousness and cognition. Lily Bart makes this passage. She responds ethically beyond her self toward a place prior to being, yet only traced within an ontological being in the here and now. Modifying Irigaray, perhaps one way to attempt to designate this place is that of "being which is not one,"[18] for in this absolutely prior priority to being, alterity has not yet been thematized as sex/gender difference. It marks a time beyond and out of time, in which actions of the human are pure reflections of the potential within human being. This is prior, then, to the thematic of Eden, in which already is the body sexed and female actions gendered and marked as translations within being, replete with aberration. Persecuted by alterity through the difference of being facing her identity, Lily employs chloral, "a queer-acting drug," to read the traces beyond their signification within ontology. In terms of gender and feminism, then, Lily's final events mark her failure to reconstruct gendered identity in any radical way. According to this discourse, Lily dies. In one convinced of a certain relation between being and an otherwise than being with a necessary priority, Lily rather moves beyond ontology and the manifestation to presence, which traces a more complex construction, a queer construction, of gender and the language bringing it to be.

The final scenes of the novel are unique in the sense that they move toward what is too queer for words. After meeting Nettie Struther and holding the baby in her arms, Lily reflects that Nettie had reached the "central truth of existence" (II, 13, 248), implied as love and safety, even after a certain disclosure of being, figured here as the openness of all past secrets. To this I would also add the less family-specific act of love, that of "human fellowship" encountered by Lily with Nettie and her baby, which takes "the mortal chill from her heart" (II, 13, 246). That night, as she drifts off to sleep under the influence of the queer-acting drug, Lily feels "Nettie Struther's child lying on her arm . . . [and] a gentle penetrating thrill of warmth and pleasure" (II, 13, 251). Immediately following, "she said to herself that there was something she must tell Selden, some word she had found that should make life clear between them. She tried to repeat the word, which lingered vague and luminous on the far edge of thought" (II, 13, 251). One could argue that in her final moments of life, the central truth of existence for Lily Bart comes as a longing for maternity and a loving connection within heterosexual pair bonding. As far as any argument concerning gendered identity goes, this reading would seem to deflate some of the more radical status of this text. But I would suggest that the non-presence of the child and the un-articulated word render the possibility of an apotheosis of maternity and heterosexual bonding as two mainstays in the patriarchal construction of women as quite queer.

In this final scene, Lily lies at the threshold, not just of consciousness and unconsciousness, but of being and beyond. As a scene of fundamental ontological trouble, the figures we are given trace the possibility of being read otherwise. The image rendered is a queer manifestation of appearance with non-presence, of Lily reaching out to hold a child that is not hers and not there. Maternity, here, is less traditional than proverbial, as a caring for that which is wholly in need, a reaching out in the embrace to carry an other that cannot exist on its own. The fecundity of this embrace exceeds the thematic of an actual child and reaches beyond to the stranger in her being that persecutes the self-centered and commodified identity of femininity. In this sense, the scene of embracing an other of being on the threshold of cognition and existing only in a queer manifestation moves further beyond Lily's earlier scene of embracing an other figure of feminine identity during ontological crisis, the reaching out to Gerty Farish (I, 14, 133). As companion pieces, these two scenes suggest a tension threshold between an ontic reaching out in need and a more prior giving over of the self to an other (in) being. As she moves into the queer space beyond what can be fully presented, and, therefore, beyond the self of feminine identity, Lily's reaching out speaks more of an abundance overflowing any particular construction of feminine identity, to the soul of being human itself. If the image of the child calls forth a fecundity of being, the non-present coming of the not hers from nowhere of this child also suggests that the other to whom the self of identity responds is the other (in) being, an embrace of self dis-covered, a figuring of a self other than itself to which one responds prior to any choice from cognition or decision as such. This act reaches out beyond being to the child of birth who is prior to being in the here and now. Any image of maternity that this scene might suggest is not a manifestation of Lily's nature. "Rather than a nature, earlier than nature, immediacy is this vulnerability, this maternity, this pre-birth or pre-nature,"[19] which John Llewelyn retranslates as the "pre-natal."[20]

In ethical terms, what is being performed here is an ethics of self dis-covery possible within ontology as its passage beyond being and its thematizations. In dis-covering the self, reaching out to the soul, responding to the "I," otherwise than of identity and identicality – the "I" of Illeity, according to Levinas – Lily moves in

that direction of the "I know not whence," of that which comes without showing itself, of the nonphenomenon and, consequently, of the non-present, of a past that was never a present, of an order to which I am subjected before hearing it or that I hear in my own saying. . . . But this singular obedience, without agreement or understanding, this allegiance prior to any oath – responsibility prior to engagement – is, precisely, the *other-in-the-same*, inspiration, prophecy – the pneuma of the soul.[21]

Not ironically but necessarily, what closes this scene and ostensibly the text is pure disclosure, "something she must tell Selden, some word she had found that should make life clear between them. She tried to repeat the word, which lingered vague and luminous on the far edge of thought" (II, 13, 251). "Thought of the word faded" (II, 13, 251) as she passes beyond. How the unarticulated word that becomes an unthinkable word signifies as Lily moves beyond can be traced in a couple of related ways. It is at once the call of alterity prior to and constitutive of being that cannot ever be repeated as *is*, but can only be rendered as the mute appeal of the displaced and unplaceable soul of the ontological self. Yet it is also the mute arch-word of a dis-covered self to an other, a word whose purity as saying can only be said as "beloved," tracing through Eros, figuring sexed bodies, the for-the-other constitution of being whose priority can only persecute (in) ontology. Only beyond being can language as word *say* but not *be said* to the other, which is a communication as passing between. "In the silence there passed between them the word which made all clear" (II, 14, 256). From beyond being comes the pure saying of connection, communication as passage, the one-for-the-other sociality of the human prior to ontic constructions of sex/gender difference within being. "My irreplaceability is therefore conferred, delivered, 'given,' one can say, by death."[22]

Allow me to anticipate an anxiety which may emerge from the assumption that the only way a woman can discover herself is to die, or that to call a kind of self-discovery that demands death ethical is anywhere from useless to sick. This kind of reaction would have to have read Lily's *"Beyond!"* straight, which is to approach only the front of the tapestry, or the text as plot. To do so is to miss the *significance*, and as such the *signifyingness* of this text, particularly of Book II. Given the social economy about which Wharton is writing, the significance of this book wields a defiance against its ostensible plot events. May "death" not be thought non-negatively, yet still signify differently, even within ontological discourse? Perhaps Lacanian discourse is more enabling here, with the final scene bringing Levinas and Lacan to the threshold of each other. Can the final events of *The House of Mirth* be read as dramatizing the ex-sistence of Woman, precisely as she no longer exists? She is other in social terms, because she is not in a relation with men, and has, it could be argued, given up on men as the relay to a relation with the phallus. Might the writing of the check for nine thousand dollars be read as precisely the moment in which she wields her own resources? Socially speaking, this *indecent* expenditure attempts to mark, in Lily's terms, decency in a mode that is insignificant to the economy of relations between men and women. It removes any debt, so to speak, to the phallus.

Would she not be characterized now as *hommosexuelle?* "She loves men, she loves like a man, and her desire is structured in fantasy like his."[23] This is another reason why the final scenes of the novel need to be thought in terms of that night with Gerty

Farish: queer as *hommosexuelle.* The link to the dream of the child is that of a *jouissance* that is fulfilled apart from a relation to the phallus. The link to the scene with Selden is that both communicate (love) absolutely, marking their desire as functioning in completely parallel ways. There is, then, no representation, particularly of the difference of woman, as the lack of representation of the word might be read as suggesting. The move *"Beyond!"* to the Other side that is hers comes necessarily with the "death" of Lily Bart, now rendered as a shell, materiality, commodity form of woman. I can have no pathos for the order of this death.

NOTES

1. Here and throughout, I mean ethics in the sense theorized by Emmanuel Levinas in his *Totality and Infinity: An Essay on Exteriority,* trans. Alphonso Lingis (Pittsburgh: Duquesne University Press, 1969), and in *Otherwise than Being or Beyond Essence,* trans. Alphonso Lingis (The Hague: Martinus Nijhoff, 1981).

2. John Llewelyn, *Emmanuel Levinas: The Genealogy of Ethics* (London: Routledge, 1995), 4.

3. Emmanuel Levinas, *Totality and Infinity: An Essay on Exteriority,* trans. Alphonso Lingis (Pittsburgh: Duquesne University Press, 1969), 284.

4. Given that Lily poses as Sir Joshua Reynolds's portrait of Mrs. Lloyd, it is probably more than coincidental that Wharton's rhetoric here emulates that of Sir Joshua Reynold's *Discourses on Art.* Wharton claims for the eye of the viewer of a *tableau* what Reynolds claims for the eye of a painter – that it must move from the particular in order to construct the general truth of nature, so much so that "painting is not only not to be considered as an imitation, operating by deception, but that it is, and ought to be, in many points of view, and strictly speaking, no imitation at all of external nature." Sir Joshua Reynolds, *Discourses on Art,* ed. Robert R. Wark (New Haven: Yale University Press, 1975), 232. Citing *Macbeth,* Reynolds claims that "the mind is to be transported, as Shakespeare expresses it, *beyond the ignorant present,* [sic] to ages past" (235–6). Macbeth I.v. 57 "beyond / This ignorant present."

5. Candace Waid includes a succinct and interesting history of the popularity and controversy of *tableaux vivants* in her book *Edith*

Wharton's Letters from the Underworld: Fictions of Women and Writing (Chapel Hill: University of North Carolina Press, 1991).

6. Emmanuel Levinas, "Truth of Disclosure and Truth of Testimony," in *Emmanuel Levinas: Basic Philosophical Writings*, ed. Adriaan T. Peperzak, Simon Critchley, and Robert Bernasconi (Bloomington: Indiana University Press, 1996), 99.

7. Ibid., 98.

8. For an analysis of the gift in these terms, see Jacques Derrida, *Given Time. 1: Counterfeit Money*, trans. Peggy Kamuf (Chicago: University of Chicago Press, 1992), and *The Gift of Death*, trans. David Wills (Chicago: University of Chicago Press, 1995).

9. Selden's Republic of the Spirit is quite a capitalistic and parasitic little republic, if what affords the possibility of seeing the "eternal harmony" of "the real" is not only the lavish expenditure of wealth needed to mount the *tableaux* and to make art (Morpeth and Silverton are all part of this system), but also the structure of cognition that runs this state of mind. Interestingly, Selden's Republic of the Spirit is similar to what John Barrell terms Reynolds's "Republic of Taste," in which people gain citizenship when they ascend to and assume the conventions of art's sensibilities. See John Barrell, *The Political Theory of Painting from Reynolds to Hazlitt* (New Haven: Yale University Press, 1986), particularly the introduction, "A Republic of Taste," and the chapter on Reynolds. For a superb reading of Reynold's *Discourses* in terms of "taste" and convention, see Karen Valihora, "A Genealogy of Common Sense: Judgment in Eighteenth-Century Literature and Philosophy" Ph.D. dissertation, Yale University, 2000). The economy of the Republic of the Spirit functions similarly to that of Lily's New York, only here intellectuality is as much the commodity as beauty or money.

10. Levinas, *Otherwise*, 46–7.

11. Ibid., 47–8.

12. Levinas, "Truth," 102.

13. René Descartes, *Meditations on First Philosophy, with Selections from the Objections and Replies*, trans. John Cottingham, introd. Bernard Williams (Cambridge: Cambridge University Press, 1986), 68.

14. Perhaps not entirely "nothing." In the structure of the cogito, with its singularity of the mind in its ability to confirm Being, there is the barest trace belying the possibility that the one of Being is constituted in a relation for the other. According to Levinas, the for-the-other constitution of the one of Being is certainly synchronized in the thematic of the cogito, but in the separation and singularity

of the "thinking" from the body, what is also shown is a certain "unintelligibility of incarnation. . . . But this impossibility of being together is the trace of the diachrony of the-one-for-the-other. That is, it is the trace of *separation* in the form of inwardness, and of the for-the-other in the form of responsibility. Identity here takes form not by a self-confirmation, but, as a signification of the-one-for-the-other, by deposing of oneself, a deposing which is the incarnation of the subject, or the very possibility of giving, of dealing signifyingness" (Levinas, *Otherwise*, 79). Less susceptible to witnessing the trace structure of signification, the traditional reception of the cogito rather prioritizes self-constitution and singularity.

15. Levinas, "Truth," 107.

16. Franz Rosenzweig, *The Star of Redemption*, trans. William W. Hallo, from the second edition of 1930 (Notre Dame: University of Notre Dame Press, 1970), 62–8.

17. To thematize this stance, which, therefore, cannot totalize its existence but can at least trace its possibility, is to follow, for example, the defiance of Israel as it accepts the law at Horeb. *Na'aseh v'nishma*: we will do and we will hear, doing before cognition. When faced with the alterity of God and God's word, ethical response to alterity is just that, response prior to and other than within an economy of cognition and the self's appropriation. As Emmanuel Levinas insists, to act before hearkening in this context is not a naiveté, nor is it even tempted by the temptation of knowing the rigor involved in such an act, which does not even partake of decision. Emmanuel Levinas, "The Temptation of Temptation," in his *Nine Talmudic Readings*, trans. Annette Aronowicz (Bloomington: Indiana University Press, 1994), 42.

18. See Luce Irigaray, *The Sex Which Is Not One*, trans. Catherine Porter (Ithaca: Cornell University Press, 1985).

19. Levinas, *Otherwise*, 75.

20. Llewelyn, *Levinas*, 146.

21. Levinas, "Truth," 106.

22. Derrida, *Gift*, 41.

23. Bruce Fink, *The Lacanian Subject: Between Language and Jouissance* (Princeton: Princeton University Press, 1995), 119. See also Jacques Lacan, *On Feminine Sexuality, The Limits of Love and Knowledge*, trans. Bruce Fink. *The Seminar of Jacques Lacan*, Book XX: Encore 1972–1973, ed. Jacques-Alain Miller (New York: Norton, 1998).

5

A Mole in the House of the Modern

LYNNE TILLMAN

Edith Wharton's passion for architecture was foundational, evidenced by her very first book, *The Decoration of Houses*, a work of nonfiction.[1] Wharton disdained the merely decorative in rooms and buildings, as she disdained it in her fiction. Her writing is severe, deliberate in its attacks and restraints, and lives in every detail and in the structure. Wharton's novels and stories move from small moments to big ones (she manages to merge the two), from openness of opportunity and hope, to inhibition and tragic limitation, from life's transitory pleasures and possibilities, to its dull and sharp pains and immobilizations. Traps and entrapment, psychological and societal, life's dead ends become the anxious terminals for Wharton's literary search for freedom and pleasure. (In her book, pleasure is freedom's affect.)

The architect Wharton is always conscious of the larger structure, with her meaning central in each scene. She meticulously furnishes a room, so that all the pieces and lines in it function as emotional or psychological props, conditions, or obstacles. Like cages or containers, her interiors keep characters in a place, often an internalized place. They enter rooms, meet, sit, talk, then Wharton lets them find the walls, the limits. She observes them in houses or on the street in chance meetings, and they fix each other – the gaze is her métier – to a moment in time, a truth (about the other or themselves), to a seat in the social theater. Everything that happens happens with effect, building her edifice. Wharton selected her words with a scalpel, as if with or without them her patient would live, die; she was precise in her renderings, otherwise the construction might fall, and other such metaphors. Her writing is never labored, though. Yet nothing's

133

simple, or simply an object, and never just an ornament. The ornament is redolent and may even be causal. (Think of *The Bunner Sisters*, the poor women whose fate hung on the repair of a timepiece. A twisted tale, but then Wharton is perverse, and sophisticated and surprising in her perverseness.)

Wharton's stately, measured rhythms let the reader linger over a sentence, then move along languidly. One may be stopped dead by some piece of psychological astuteness, a blunt idea, by brutal clarity, or staggered by an almost excessive, because perfect, image. Slowly, Wharton draws beautiful portraits, deceptive pictures. (I sometimes wonder if Wharton ever felt rushed by anything, then I remember Morton Fullerton and her love letters to him, that rush late in her life.) Beautiful language serves – like tea, an elegant service – ironic and difficult ends. It lures one into a network of sinister complications and, transformed, beauty leads to dreariness and viciousness. The reader will be torn by the loss of that plenitude, by failure, by hopelessness.

But Wharton is economical about elegance, stringent about lushness, display, every embellishment. Rarely extravagant. Maybe it's because she understood position and space, knew she didn't really have much room, no room for profligacy. She couldn't run from reality, even if she wanted to (and I think she did), so she had no room to waste, certainly no words to waste. The inessential might obscure the clarity she sought. She wouldn't let herself go, let her writing go. She understood the danger, she understood any form of complicity. Her often privileged protagonists fatally conspire with society against themselves, become common prey to its dictates, helpless to disown or resist what they despise in themselves and in it. Wharton was profoundly aware that, seen by others, she was free to do what she pleased, a privileged woman dangling the world on a rich string. And she wrote, perhaps explained, early on in *The House of Mirth*, Lily Bart "was so evidently the victim of the civilization which had produced her, that the links of her bracelet seemed like manacles chaining her to her fate" (I, 1, 8).

* * * * *

I have sometimes thought that a woman's nature is like a great house full of rooms; there is the hall, through which everyone passes in going in and out; the drawing room, where one receives formal visits; the sitting room, where the members of the family come and go as they list; but beyond that, far beyond, are other rooms, the handles of whose doors perhaps are never turned; no one knows the way to them, no one knows whither they lead; and in the innermost room, the holy of holies, the soul sits alone and waits for a doorstep that never comes.

The Fullness of Life (1891)

In Wharton's scheme, Lily Bart's fate was to be beautiful, to become poor and unmarriageable, and to die a suicide, a tragic heroine. Like bread crumbs, Wharton scatters clues to Lily's predicament. "[S]he likes being good and I like being happy," Lily says of poor Gerty Farish to Lawrence Selden (I, 1, 8). Some of the clues correspond to Selden's grand idea, proposed once to Lily, that there is a "republic of the spirit" she might enter (I, 6, 55). Lily's conflict – her wish for freedom but her sense "that I never had any choice" (I, 6, 55) – conspires to keep her from the independent or idiosyncratic life Selden represents. (His republic of the spirit is an imaginary structure, perhaps the house of mirth itself.)

Wharton's use of architecture operates in the traditional way – as built structure, as expression of the symbolic order, as place, as evidence of the hierarchical order – but it is exercised for fictive ends. The novel begins in a terminal, Grand Central Station, and terminates in a rented room. The "house" is first a capacious, modern public building, a place anyone may enter and pass through, and last a cramped space open to the public but required only by the poor. Lily journeys, like Richard II, from bigness to smallness, from a magnificent building that seems infinite – kingdom, modern world – to a small rented room of desperate finitude – cell, deathbed. Space and place change with Lily Bart, or change her.

* * * * *

Lawrence Selden makes Lily happy or sad whenever they meet. It is Selden whom Lily encounters by chance in Grand Central

135

Station, and it's Selden who finds Lily dead at the novel's end. His presence frames Lily's life, ghosts and subverts it, as the rooms, scenes, and encounters Wharton sets Lily in structure it. What the reader knows of Lily's thoughts about her impossible position are gleaned primarily in her discussions with Selden, her foil and confidante. Selden is a fitting comrade, a modern flawed hero or antihero. He arouses the dubious sprite fortune and its reversals, and with its partner, hope and possibility, plagues Lily. No one underwrites Lily's essential placelessness, or lovelessness, more than Selden.

Wharton had a keen interest in ghost stories and the supernatural, and Selden flits through *The House of Mirth* as if it were a Gothic tale and he were its elusive hero. Selden is a haunted and haunting figure who magnifies Lily's unfitness and increasing inappropriateness whenever he appears. Her double in drag, he even impedes her so-called progress with other suitors, fulfilling his double-agent, phantom-lover mission as the budding star in a magnificent series of plot points. His last appearance at Lily's bedside makes her death more pointedly tragic and beautiful, since we see her through his shattered vision. At that deadly moment, Selden becomes a character – or an ornament – Wharton might have borrowed from Poe.

The House of Mirth was originally titled "A Moment's Ornament"; Lily Bart could have been its temporary decoration. Though, from Lily's point of view, the occasional ornament could have been Selden. But then Wharton enjoyed symmetries. Her house, the Mount, in Lenox, Massachusetts, which she designed and had built, has three front doors, one of them fake; Wharton wanted the facade to be symmetrical. Selden is symmetrical to Lily and does balance her, even as he unbalances her. (Symmetry, to Wharton, "the answering of one part to another, may be defined as the sanity of decoration" [*Decoration*, 7].) The uncoupled couple form a double-faced statue that articulates Wharton's comprehension of how women's changed, conflictual desires are met by changed, conflicted men. Both are, in a way, misfits, though Selden's eccentricity and inappropriateness, including his bachelorhood, have value, while Lily's spinsterhood and virginity daily lose theirs.

* * * * *

Wharton's enclosures house conflicts and conflicted characters, created not just by ordinary walls. The author constructs walls, limits, that are both real and metaphorical. Wharton's central and most sustained trope, architecture always alludes to Lily's physical or mental space, her environment or psychological condition. The decor – couches, paintings, fireplaces, bric-a-brac – becomes evidence of the state in which she exists or of the character of the characters she meets.

[Mrs. Dorset] could have been crumpled up and run through a ring, like the sinuous draperies she affected. . . . she was like a disembodied spirit who took up a great deal of room. (I, 2, 21–2)

There was nothing new to Lily in these tokens of a studied luxury; but, though they formed a part of her atmosphere, she never lost her sensitiveness to their charm. Mere display left her with a sense of superior distinction; but she felt an affinity to all the subtler manifestations of wealth. (I, 4, 34)

Look at a boy like Ned Silverton – he's really too good to to be used to refurbish anybody's social shabbiness. (I, 6, 56–7)

The exterior suggests the interior or, rather, is the manifestation, the visible order, of an inner world.

Since architecture also defines space by what is not built and what lies outside, the trope allows Wharton to delineate the unbounded, permeable relationship between outside and inside, the flow and inevitable transmission between the so-called inner life and outer life. Lily contends with the limits of public life and space, with propriety and sensibility, with street life, the places without walls that are bounded and limited, to women.

All good architecture and good decoration (which it must never be forgotten *is only interior architecture*) must be based on rhythm and logic. (*Decoration*, 13)

For Lily Bart, leaving rooms and being on the street is hazardous; it's when many of her most devastating and decisive encounters occur. Leaving Selden's apartment, she accidentally meets Mr. Rosedale in front of the Benedick (bachelor) Apartments. She tells a lie that propels the novel's story – and her undoing – into motion. Lily instantly realizes her error. (Rosedale's appearance has been foreshadowed by an unkempt charwoman on the Benedick stairs, who unsettles Lily and with whom Lily compares herself. The charwoman also returns to plague her, blackmail her.)

Why must a girl pay so dearly for her least escape from routine? Why could one never do a natural thing without having to screen it behind a structure of artifice? (I, 2, 19)

Her comings and goings are not easy, she doesn't make smooth exits; and there are certainly no escapes.

Ironically, Lily identifies with the man who can undo her, Simon Rosedale, a noveau riche Jewish businessman initially sketched by Wharton with the brush of conventional anti-Semitism. He is, like Lily, "a novelty" (I, 2, 16). She "understood his motives, for her own course was guided by as nice calculations" (I, 2, 16). Within a very few pages, Wharton serves up two male characters, dissimilar to each other and to her, as well as a dissimilar female, against whom to judge Lily. All balance our view of her, creating a kind of symmetry or the rhythm and logic fundamental to Wharton's idea of design in architecture and fiction.

Later in the novel, "as [Selden and Van Alstyne] walked down Fifth Avenue [to Mrs. Fisher's] the new architectural developments of that versatile thoroughfare invited Van Alstyne's comments" (I, 14, 126). On their way, talking, "they were just beneath the wide white facade, with its rich restraint of line, which suggested the clever corseting of a redundant figure" (I, 14, 126). (Wharton may be commenting upon her techniques for outlining the "redundant" manners and modes she must contend with in society and in constructing, "corseting," her fictions.) Then Van Alstyne remarks about Mrs. Bry's architect:

What a clever chap . . . how he takes his client's measure! He has put the whole of Mrs. Bry in his use of the composite order! (I, 14, 126)

Architecture, to Wharton's thinking, can reveal the whole of a character. When Van Alstyne and Selden reach the Trenor house, Van Alstyne reports it's empty and remarks offhandedly that Mrs. Trenor is away.

The house loomed obscure and uninhabited; only an oblong gleam above the door spoke of provisional occupancy. (I, 14, 127)

At this moment, whose consequences also loom obscure, Lily is discovered in the doorway with Gus Trenor. She has just fought him off and is leaving. Her provisional presence, not inside, not outside, endangers her. Compromised, in the wrong place at the wrong time, seen by Selden, whose heart has recently turned more decisively toward her, and by her relative, Van Alstyne, her fortune is immediately reversed. But her name is never used; she has entered the realm of the unspeakable.

Wharton deploys a discourse on houses, about how an architect (maker/writer) can expose the character of the persons whose house he designs, to position Lily. When she appears in a place where she should not be, her presence there says something about her. Though this was not her design, many of the things Lily does are designed, and many that appear designing and manipulative are not. Ineluctably, Lily becomes ensnared in patterns not of her making that are not provisional enough.

* * * * *

To conform to a style, then, is to accept those rules of proportion which the artistic experience of centuries has established as the best, while within those limits allowing free scope to the individual requirements which must inevitably modify every house or room adapted to the use and convenience of its occupants. (*Decoration*, 15)

True originality consists not in a new manner but in a new vision. (*Writing*, 17)[2]

The distrust of technique and the fear of being unoriginal – both symptoms of a certain lack of creative abundance – are in truth leading to pure anarchy in fiction. (*Writing*, 15)

In *The Decoration of Houses* (1897) and *The Writing of Fiction* (1924), Wharton argues for conformity to style and tradition against originality for its own sake. The rhythm and logic of the past must be observed or at least taken into account and regarded, if not entirely followed. Wharton even claims that stream of consciousness and slice of life are the same idea; stream

139

of consciousness is slice of life "relabelled" (*Writing*, 12). Her aesthetics and views on morality and convention form the underlying arguments in the novel and contain within them the seeds of conflict planted and harvested in Lily Bart.

Enshrined in Lily is a contest between new and old, tradition, innovation, and the hazards of change. On the first page of the novel, Wharton efficiently marks her territory when Selden thinks to himself: "There was nothing new about Lily Bart, yet he could never see her without a faint movement of interest" (I, 1, 5). To him she was so "radiant" she was "more conspicuous than a ballroom" (I, 1, 5). (The scale is striking, so disproportionate.) But not bold enough or too principled to marry for money and live anyway she chooses, she cannot strike out on her own and exist on her meager income, like Gerty Farish. She is not a new woman. Wharton does not allow her a wholly new manner, which the author disdains, but she also does not provide Lily with vision for a new life.

(Lily is more like a new woman manqué. It's as if Wharton invented her to put on trial and test her principle of "conform[ing] to a style . . . [that] artistic experience of centuries has established as the best, while within those limits allowing free scope to the individual requirements." How one holds to tradition and style and discovers within them "free scope" is at the crux of Wharton's contradictory, ongoing argument with the modernists and the social order.)

Lily contains within her traces and pieces of the old order and longings for the new. Wharton drops Lily between the two worlds, on the frontier, where no place is home or safe. Habitually, Lily pays the price for not being able to realize a new way and for needing the largesse of others whom she despises or for whom she has contempt.

That cheap originality which finds expression in putting things to uses for which they were not intended is often confounded with individuality; whereas the latter consists not in an attempt to be different from other people at the cost of comfort, but in the desire to be comfortable in one's own way, even though it be the way of a monotonously large majority. It seems easier to most people to arrange a room like some one else's than to analyze and express their own needs. (*Decoration*, 19–20)

Lily's difference from the "monotonously large majority" hangs her on a cross constructed from an opposition between novelty and individuality. She feels superior and wants to discover and "express [her] own needs," as Selden does. She must find a way to "use" herself, not as a "cheap experiment" but in the intended way. But there is no intended way, not for her.

* * * * *

Men, in these matters, are less exacting than women, because their demands, besides being simpler, are uncomplicated by the feminine tendency to want things because other people have them, rather than to have things because they are wanted. But it must never be forgotten that every one is unconsciously tyrannized over by the wants of others. . . . The unsatisfactory relations of some people with their rooms are often to be explained in this way. They have still in their blood the traditional uses to which these rooms were put in times quite different from the present. . . . To go to the opposite extreme and discard things because they are old-fashioned is equally unreasonable. (*Decoration*, 19–20)

Desire is a strange brew, Wharton knew, concocted of the desires of others. Her psychological acumen suffuses *The House of Mirth*, in which Lily is "unconsciously tyrannized over by the wants of others." Lily has "in her blood" the uses for which she was made but is unwilling to go to "the opposite extreme" and "discard things" because they are "old-fashioned."

Once more the haunting sense of physical ugliness was intensified by her mental depression, so that each piece of the offending furniture seemed to thrust forth its most aggressive angle. (I, 9, 86)

Lily does want to get rid of ugly things. The effects of physical ugliness – disproportion – and mental depression intermingle in her. Their symmetry or dissymmetry serves Wharton's notion of the interior as inextricable from the exterior. Lily's internal conflicts are displayed in the outer world, where she is a beautiful but tormented trophy in its display case. Her inner struggles show themselves as much by what she does not do as by what she does.

It must be pure bliss to arrange the furniture just as one likes, and give all the horrors to the ashman. If I could only do over my aunt's drawing room I know I should be a better woman. (I, 1, 8)

141

Lily's longing to clean out her aunt's room is a wish to change herself, to throw out her own horrors. In a better room, she might become better – setting and place affect character. But Lily can't throw out the horrors, she cannot change the conditions in which she lives that have made her the kind of woman she is. When she strikes out against convention or her interests, by spending time with Selden and avoiding her rich, boring suitor, Percy Gryce, her revolt takes the shape of inaction, temporizing. She may want to remove horrors but she does not act or cannot. Cleaning her aunt's room of horrors could also be another clever reference to the Gothic, but from the Gothic, which preceded Freud, with its insistence on the darkness in human beings and the cauldron of murky, unconscious desires that drive behavior, other ideas march in. They enter through a side door – call it the unarticulated or the unconscious – of Wharton's subtle fiction.

* * * * *

. . . she was not meant for mean and shabby surroundings, for the squalid compromises of poverty. Her whole being dilated in an atmosphere of luxury, it was the background she required, the only climate she could breathe in. But the luxury of others was not what she wanted. . . . Now she was beginning to chafe at the obligations it imposed, to feel herself a mere pensioner on the splendor which had once seemed to belong to her. There were even moments when she was conscious of having to pay her way. (I, 3, 23)

Lily pays by being charming and by trying to keep her reputation intact. A twentieth-century Clarissa, who even fights off a rape, Lily's chastity is a series of questions. Purity? Property? Repression? Inhibition? Architecture is, among other things, about bodies living within structures built for bodies by bodies. Lily is subject, even prey, to assaults within two kinds of structures – external or social and internal or psychological. The exterior holds, conditions, and is manifested in the interior, interiority inhabited and penetrated by the social. (If houses and ornaments are mated, psychologies are married to societies.)

She had always hated her room at Mrs. Peniston's – its ugliness, its impersonality, the fact that nothing in it was really hers. To a torn heart uncomforted by human nearness a room may open almost human arms, and the being to whom no four walls mean more than any others, is, at such hours, expatriate everywhere. (I, 13, 118)

She had tried to mitigate this charmless background by a few frivolous touches . . . but the futility of the attempt struck her as she looked about the room. What a contrast to the subtle elegance of the setting she had pictured for herself – an apartment which should surpass the complicated luxury of her friends' surroundings by the whole extent of that artistic sensibility which made herself feel their superior. (I, 9, 86)

Lily wants her accommodations to fit her sense of superiority. But they usually don't. She may even want a house or room, with its "almost human arms," more than a man and marriage, a desire for which society traditionally punishes women. Living at her aunt's, Mrs. Peniston – penal, penurious, penis – Lily must sleep and dream in a bedroom that's "as dreary as a prison" (I, 9, 86). Since Wharton's prisons are real spaces and metaphors, Lily's mind and body are trapped not only in dreary rooms but also in the society whose customs shape her.

* * * * *

The survival of obsolete customs in architecture, which makes the study of sociology so interesting, has its parallel in the history of architecture. (*Decoration*, 5)

Excremental things are all too intimately and inseparably bound up with sexual things. . . . The genitals themselves have not undergone the development of the rest of the human form in the direction of beauty; they have retained their animal cast; and so even today love, too, is in essence as animal as it ever was.[3]

Sigmund Freud and Edith Wharton were contemporaries. They lived during approximately the same years, Freud from 1856 to 1939, Wharton 1866 to 1937. Freud was as interested in archeology as Wharton was in architecture; it was foundational for his thought. He mined it for metaphors and used it as analogues to human psychology. Wharton obviously had an interest in psychology, though it's unlikely she read Freud. She was aware of him, as every educated person would have been then, and wrote in a letter to Bernard Berenson, "Please ask Mary not to

143

befuddle her with Freudianism and all its jargon."[4] Though she eschewed Freud's "jargon," Wharton understood the terms, the ground on which she built her characters. Wharton had a sophisticated understanding of psychology, and her treatment and development of Lily Bart shows her exploring some issues that Freud did. Differently, of course.

Beneath the customs of society lie what the Gothic, and ghost stories, point to: human anxieties and fears, needs and motives driven by desires and instincts not governable by reason. The vicissitudes of sex and sexuality, duty and morality, wreak havoc on Wharton's characters, whether in this novel, *The Age of Innocence*, or *Madame de Treymes*. Wharton is the poet of oppression and repression, and, attending to her project, she doesn't permit Lily to have the brilliant life she wants. Instead, she presents her with obstacles. Freud might call them neuroses. Whatever one calls them, "things" are in the way of Lily Bart's ability to thrive.

The preciousness of Lily's reputation reflects the irrational foundations of her world. Taboos about virginity mark both so-called primitive and civilized societies. They mask, Freud theorized, universal human fears about female sexuality and sexuality itself. Wharton's female characters dwell and flail about in a troubled, transitional period (a very long moment that continues to the present). Like Freud, Wharton was nurtured in a Victorian culture and then lived on into a newer, modern world. Like him, she studied the psychological effects on people resistant to, and transformed by, great cultural and social changes. (In *The Mother's Recompense*, the mother flees her marriage, abandons her young daughter, for her lover. Years later, the daughter, whom she hasn't seen since she ran away, will become engaged to that same man. It's a cautionary Oedipal tale about what can happen if women chase after their desires. When the social order is overturned, duty and obligation ignored for siren freedom, Wharton intimates, incest is a possibility.)

Seated under the cheerless blaze of the drawing room chandelier – Mrs. Peniston never lit the lamps unless there was "company" – Lily seemed to watch her own figure retreating down vistas of neutral-tinted dulness to a middle-age like Grace Stepney's. (I, 9, 80)

Inside this narrow world of prohibition and inhibition, Lily's possibilities are limited. If Selden embodies Lily's hopes, her utopian vision, Grace Stepney personifies her fears of the nightmarish future – poverty, spinsterhood, social ugliness. The fear of turning into Grace alarms Lily as much as Selden's freedom entices her.

> Ah, there's the difference – a girl must, a man may if he chooses. . . . Your coat's a little shabby – but who cares? It doesn't keep people from asking you to dine. If I were shabby no one would have me: a woman is asked out as much for her clothes as herself. . . .Who wants a dingy woman? We are expected to be pretty and well-dressed until we drop – and if we can't keep it up alone, we have to go into partnership. (I, 1, 12)

* * * * *

The social constraints for women are as clear as the crystal in the houses Wharton describes. But she proposes less obvious or visible constraints. Rarely insistent or repetitive, she is both about Lily's beauty and her terror of dinginess. (Two sides of the same coin, they may constitute her fatal flaw.) Lily's dread – "who wants a dingy woman?" – renders her incapable of happiness, even of living within her means. Even if one supposes one understands how Lily's beauty works – as surface or appearance, as a manifestation of the sublime, as her difference from others, as artistic perfection and imperfection (the human golden bowl) – dinginess is still trickier, more obscure and difficult to grasp. But both refer to the liminal, mostly unseen relationship between interiors and exteriors.

Beauty and dinginess, beauty and the beast, depend upon each other. Dinginess isn't brilliant, sublime, perfect, but dirty, tainted, dark, discolored, worn, or spoiled, used, and disgusting. (The word "dingy" may come from the word "dinghy," a small boat or vessel that sails by the side of larger vessels.) Lily's mother instills the terror of it in her. Mrs. Bart's greatest "reproach" to her husband is that he expected her to become dingy or "live like a pig" (I, 3, 26), one of Freud's animals. (Anality comes to mind.) Treated with indifference and contempt, Mr. Bart's a cash machine to his wife and to Lily, who has more sympathy for him.

After he loses his money, his failure and inadequacy in Mrs. Bart's eyes are made complete when he dies and leaves them poor, ruined.

After two years of hungry roaming, Mrs. Bart had died – of a deep disgust. She had hated dinginess, and it was her fate to be dingy. Her visions of a brilliant marriage for Lily had faded after the first year. (I, 3, 30)

To Miss Bart, as to her mother, acquiescence in dinginess was evidence of stupidity; and there were moments when, in the consciousness of her own power to look and be so exactly what the occasion required, she almost felt that other girls were plain and inferior from choice. (I, 8, 70)

Mrs. Peniston's opulent interior was at least not externally dingy. But dinginess is a quality that assumes all manner of disguises; and Lily soon found it was as latent in the expensive routine of her aunt's life as in the makeshift existence of a continental pension. (I, 3, 31)

Dinginess isn't ever simple wear and tear. Contrasted again and again to brilliance, light, the sun, glow (as if Wharton were a Manichee), the dark and dirty that Lily fears and names dinginess emanates from what she doesn't know and can't see. There's no clarity, no bright light by which to see these appalling, unconscious forces that threaten her every step. Stupidity, as dullness, is also dinginess (though for her to shine too brilliantly could attract unwanted attention and failure). But Lily is stupid before the irrational. Wharton knew everyone was.

In an extraordinary passage, Lily worries that Mrs. Peniston ("To attempt to bring her into active relation with life was like tugging at a piece of furniture which has been screwed to the floor" [I, 3, 32]) has been "too passive," has not helped her enough socially; but Lily also fears she herself has "not been passive enough" and too "eager" (I, 3, 33).

Younger and plainer girls had been married off by the dozens, and she was nine and twenty, and still Miss Bart.

She was beginning to have fits of angry rebellion against fate, when she longed to drop out of the race and make an independent life for herself. But what manner of life would it be? . . . She was too intelligent not to be honest with herself. She knew that she hated dinginess as much as her mother had hated it, and to her last breath she meant to

146

fight against it, dragging herself up again and again against its flood till she gained the bright pinnacles of success which presented such a slippery surface to her clutch. (I, 3, 33)

She fights against being ruined. It's a struggle to the death that she loses, one beyond her control, fought blindly, unconsciously. For a smart girl, Lily often acts impulsively and against her interests. But Wharton sometimes confounds the reader who is attempting to decide what is in her interest. Maybe nothing is. Even if Lily knew what her interests were, she might not be able to stop herself or control herself, for reasons she cannot know.

* * * * *

The question persists: If plainer and stupider girls could marry, why can't Lily? Marriage's promise is not just economic and social partnership, but also sexual union. Terror of sex and sexuality, of being made dingy, may be a piece of Lily's unmarriageability, inscribed in her body as attenuated virginity. Intent upon weaving surface and foundation, Wharton lets Lily's body and interior speak society's prohibitive customs and conventions.

(Imagining a character's psychology can be as "slippery" as the "bright pinnacles of success" Lily can't reach. But Wharton looks hard at Lily, as a condition, as a symptom of social injustice, restriction, inhibition, repression, oppression, as an unstable object in an uncertain structure. She scrutinizes her with a kind of clinical neutrality.

The chief difference between the merely sympathetic and the creative imagination is that the latter is two-sided, and combines with the power of penetrating into other minds that of standing far enough aloof from them to see beyond, and relate them to the whole stuff of life out of which they partially emerge. Such an all-round view can be obtained only by mounting to a height; and that height, in art, is proportioned to the artist's power of detaching one part of his imagination from the particular problem in which the rest is steeped. (*Writing*, 15)

Her very sharp pen, held high, is dipped in the ink of ambivalence – fascination, contempt, compassion, anger, fear. Like all writers, Wharton works as much from what she knows as from what she doesn't. The unconscious presents mysteries and allows pleasures, pains, and pathologies a visibility that one can't plan or control.)

Lily's unlovableness and sense of unworthiness is disguised by her beautiful, impenetrable exterior. She's valued for it alone.

One thought consoled [Mrs. Bart], and that was the contemplation of Lily's beauty. . . . It was the last asset in their fortunes. . . . She watched it jealously as if it were her own property and Lily its mere custodian . . . (I, 3, 29)

The dinginess of her present life threw into enchanting relief the exis-tence to which she felt herself entitled. To a less illuminated intelligence Mrs. Bart's counsels might have been dangerous, but Lily understood that beauty is only the raw material of conquest, and that to convert it into success other arts are required. She knew that to betray any sense of superiority was a subtler form of the stupidity her mother denounced, and it did not take her long to learn that a beauty needs more tact than the possessor of an average set of features. (I, 3, 30)

Lily can't manipulate what's inside her, her feelings about who she is or isn't. Her beauty is unassailable and absolute, no one touches it – or her. But its scale triggers alarms, calls too much attention upon her, and maybe isn't a good enough cover story. She manages it, like her intelligence, though it's inconvenient and ill-fitting – "more conspicuous than a ballroom." Lily's "passion for the appropriate" (I, 6, 51) may be oxymoronic.

* * * * *

In *The Decoration of Houses*, Wharton claims that "structure con-ditions ornament, not ornament structure" (*Decoration*, 14). Lily's an ornament that can be betrayed, deformed, in the wrong setting. Her beauty will turn ugly if nothing else around it, or within her, supports it, makes it function or harmonize with the structure that conditions it. Inappropriate and out of context, beauty can be empty, a thing, nothing but a facade, a fake. When Selden thinks he "see[s] before him the real Lily Bart," she is a *tableau vivant*, an image, "Mrs. Lloyd" of the Reynolds painting (I, 12, 106). He suddenly perceives her "divested of the trivial-ities of her little world and catching for a moment a note of that eternal harmony of which her beauty was a part" (I, 12, 106).

It's a singular moment. Lily blends in, in the right setting, and is embraced by Selden for her perfection. Selden's revery is shattered, though, when Ned Van Alstyne trivializes her, and he becomes indignant.

This was the world she lived in, these were the standards by which she was fated to be measured! Does one go to Caliban for a judgment on Miranda? (I, 12, 107)

He's sympathetic to her; but she's an idealized image. Wharton extolls her beauty in this highly artificial, artful scene. She freezes Lily and portrays her as a living picture, so there's something grotesque about it, and about her, too. She's not quite human. But Selden, an aesthete, can adore her and suspend his harsh judgment of her. He can almost love her.

Selden's no less harsh about her, and society, than she is. There's dogged reason in Wharton's pairing of these cool characters, each of whom mirrors the other's desires and lacks. The differences between them elucidate differences based on sex, but through them, Wharton plays with balancing the unbalanced sexes.

If he did not often act on the accepted social axiom that a man may go where he pleases, it was because he had long since learned that his pleasures were mainly to be found in a small group of the like-minded. But he enjoyed spectacular effects, and was not insensible to the part money plays in their production. All he asked was that the very rich live up to their calling as stage managers, and not spend their money in a dull way. (I, 12, 103–4)

Like Lily, Selden isn't rich, but unlike her he works for a living. Like Lily, he abjures dullness, appreciates beauty and the finer things, has a pronounced and cultivated sensibility, and recognizes and is repulsed by vulgarity. He feels above most people; he wants to avoid being bored. His lack of chastity isn't, of course, an obstacle. Lily often talks with him about her chances for marriage. But she rarely thinks about or mentions love. (When Lily loves and thrills, it is to rooms and places. Her sensitivity to a room and decoration is as excessive as her beauty.) One of the times love is spoken by her, though, is when she thinks about Selden.

149

[Lily] could not herself have explained the sense of buoyancy which seemed to lift and swing her above the sun-suffused world at her feet. Was it love, she wondered, or a mere fortuitous combination of happy thoughts and sensations? How much of it was owing to the spell of the perfect afternoon, the scent of the fading woods, the thought of the dulness she had fled from? Lily had no definite experience by which to test the quality of her feelings. She had several times been in love with fortunes or careers, but only once with a man. . . . If Lily recalled this early emotion it was not to compare it with that which now possessed her, the only point of comparison was the sense of lightness, of emancipation, which she remembered feeling . . . that glow of freedom; but now it was something more than blind groping of the blood. (I, 6, 52)

Earlier in the scene, Lily waits for Selden to come to her, surrounded by nature, with which she "had no real intimacy" (I, 6, 51). Nature is another one of *The House of Mirth*'s uneasier foundations. What is woman's nature? With freedom, will Lily Bart be "womanly," capable of giving herself in marriage, having babies, and conforming to social obligations? Or will she become too new, unusable?

She's been "in love with fortunes and careers, but only once with a man." Nature and love aren't natural to Lily, and she doesn't conform to feminine proscriptions that link women with nature, women with love. Lily thinks she knows Selden's nature, since it's like hers. His "air of friendly aloofness . . . [is] . . . the quality which piqued Lily's interest" (I, 6, 53). Selden's aloofness sets Lily up, off, and down. She doesn't know what to expect from him, never knows if he loves her or might be serious about marrying her.

Everything about him accorded with the fastidious element in her taste, even to the light irony with which he surveyed what seemed to her most scared. She admired him most of all, perhaps, for being able to convey as distinct a sense of superiority as the richest man she had ever met. (I, 6, 53)

She admires him for an irony that keeps him at a distance. Like her, his passions are oxymoronically reserved for the appropriate. Wharton's odd couple are dedicated to controlling themselves. But love jeopardizes control, forces one to become involuntarily subject to another, even lost in the other. Selden's suspicious of losing himself, and he's so suspicious of Lily he thinks that "even her weeping was an art." (I, 6, 58)

> That which he projects ahead of him as his ideal is merely his substitute for the lost narcissism of his childhood – the time when he was his own ideal.[5]

When Selden thought he saw the real Lily Bart, she was a living doll. Maybe he loved her most then as a lost part of himself, the illusory ideal he once imagined himself to be or have. They're both difficult characters, wary of love, looking for perfection. Not finding it in themselves or others, they don't lose themselves.

In a recent TV advertisement for a men's perfume called Contradiction, a young man declares, "I don't want her to need me, I want her to desire me. Need isn't desire." Lily needs Selden more than she desires him; Selden's idea of freedom entails being wanted, not needed. Their attraction to each other is unstable and compelling, living, dying, again and again. The contradictory logic that might make them lovers – both are ambivalent, both want freedom – is precisely what makes them unfit for each other.

* * * * *

In this thwarted romance, star-crossed lovers want to love but can't, do in some ways love themselves and each other, but also share in self-loathing, an effect, too, of narcissism. Freud wrote that loving oneself is not a "perversion but the libidinal complement to the egoism of the instinct of self-preservation, a measure of which may justifiably be attributed to every living creature" ("Narcissism," 105). Selden's self-regard appears less compromised than Lily's; she worries too much about becoming dingy. But both suffer from narcissistic wounds and lick them throughout the novel, sparing themselves the pain of further injury.

> The effect of the dependence upon the love object is to lower that feeling [of self-regard]: the lover is humble. He who loves has, so to speak, forfeited a part of his narcissism, which can only be replaced by his being loved. ("Narcissism," 120)

There is, in the act of love, a great resemblance to torture or to a surgical operation.[6]

Selden and Lily never stop preserving and defending themselves from imagined or real injuries and threats. Love – relinquishment of control – might be torture for them. When Lily visits Selden for the last time, she is finally able to articulate it.

Do you remember what you said to me once? That you could help me only by loving me? Well – you did love me for a moment; and it helped me. But the moment is gone – it was I who let it go. And one must go on living. Goodbye. (II, 12, 241)

Love's dead, but "something lived between them also. . . . it was the love his love had kindled, the passion of her soul for his" (II, 12, 241). Her idea of love colludes with Wharton's understanding of desire that arises from the desire to be desired. Even more abstractly, Lily understands that "she could not go forth and leave her old self with him; that self must indeed live on in his presence, but it must still continue to be hers" (II, 12, 241). Even when love is dead, no longer capable of causing pain, surgery – amputation – won't be allowed. Lily's fear of losing herself, giving herself up to him, certainly may be her magnificent desire to be herself. But what Wharton suggests is that her impassioned need to preserve herself at all costs may be an implacable obstacle to happiness; for it she will pay the ultimate price.

* * * * *

Not coincidentally, the most exquisite or maybe the only love scene in *The House of Mirth* is not between Selden and Lily, but between mother and child – with Lily playing the mother and becoming the child in a kind of self-love scene. (It's also the only scene in which one character holds another with passion or for any length of time.) After the devastating last meeting with Selden, Lily bumps into Nettie Crane Struthers, one of Gerty Farish's "girls," on the street.

Nettie Struther's frail envelope was now alive with hope and energy; whatever fate the future reserved for her, she would not be cast into the refuse heap without a struggle. (II, 13, 243)

Though poor, Nettie's not rubbish, not dingy. Nettie invites Lily home: "it's real warm in our kitchen" (II, 13, 244). In another of Wharton's relatively few underscorings and repetitions, she italicizes "was" in Lily's repeated thought: "It *was* warm in the kitchen" (II, 13, 244). (Warm or warmth occurs several more times in this hearth-and-home kitchen scene.) Nettie's life, though different from Lily's, has its similarities. She was about to give up, having been jilted, but unlike Lily, Nettie found a man, George, married, and had a baby. Nettie's reputation doesn't stop George from marrying her; Lily's stops everyone. Nettie's success as a traditional woman, playing traditional roles, is severely contrasted to Lily's failures, her flawed femininity and fatal unmarriageability. This extreme pairing, before Lily's suicide, seems to enunciate the author's ambivalence toward Lily and the allure and demands of femininity. And maybe it also addresses Wharton's own maternal deprivation, since through the veil of fiction one writes what one wants as much as what one doesn't.

When Lily holds Nettie's baby, at first the child

seemed as light as a pink cloud or a heap of down, but as she continued to hold it the weight increased, sinking deeper, and penetrating her with a strange sense of weakness, as though the child entered into her and became a part of herself. (II, 13, 245–6)

Wharton fashions another *tableau vivant*, a *Madonna and Child* (by Bellini, let's say), and paints the badly mothered Lily Bart into it. In a moment of devastating psychological revelation, Lily is transformed as the infant enters her. The baby becomes a lost part of her, an adult still so little, so undeveloped, she's as weak as a baby, or she is the baby.

[Nettie:] "Wouldn't it be too lovely if she grew up to be just like you?"
[Lily:] "Oh she must not do that – I should be afraid to come to see her too often." (II, 13, 246)

Now Wharton's gone Gothic again, writing a ghost story. Lily foresees her death, and, as a ghost, could return to visit the real Lily Bart, who has never actually existed. The baby could become the person she might have been, had she been loved and able to thrive. At Nettie's warm hearth, Lily's heartless mother is a spectral presence, with Lily's pathetic, beaten-down father hovering in the corner where her mother placed him. (What kind of man could Lily love after him? Or, even, could Lily really love a man after him?)

* * * * *

One may distinguish the novel of situation from that of character and manners by saying that, in the first, the persons imagined by the author almost always spring out of a vision of the situation, and are inevitably conditioned by it, whatever the genius of their creator; whereas in the larger freer form, that of character and manners (or either of the two), the author's characters are first born, and then mysteriously proceed to work out their destinies. (*Writing*, 89)

In writing and design, Wharton strove for clean lines and economy, to remove excess. Lily's excessive, a disturbance within the social structure. It's rotten, but she's a character formed inside its rooms. Lily wanted to be an original, and Wharton, conflicted and ambivalent about the new, gave her enough rope to hang herself – trapping her between the novel of situation (or circumstance and circumstantial evidence) and the novel of character. Through her imperfect heroine, Wharton proclaimed the vivacious allure of freedom, the voracious seductiveness and promise of modernity and change, with all its destructive potential, and the helplessness of individuals before the claims of blind desire. Like Freud, Wharton described, not prescribed, the conditions in which women and men lived. But she didn't allow them a talking cure, and her characters have very little room in which to negotiate happy endings.

* * * * *

Another unsettling element of modern art is that common symptom of immaturity, the dread of doing what has been done before; for though one of the instincts of youth is imitation, another, equally imperious, is that of fiercely guarding against it. (*Writing*, 17)

Original vision is never much afraid of using accepted forms [my italics]; and only the cultivated intelligence escapes the danger of regarding as intrinsically new what may be a mere superficial change, or the reversion to a discarded trick of technique. (*Writing*, 109)

There is one more thing to be said in defence of conformity to style; and that is, the difficulty of getting rid of style. Strive as we may for originality, we are hampered at every turn by an artistic tradition of over two thousand years. Does any but the most inexperienced architect really think he can ever rid himself of such an inheritance? He may mutilate or misapply the component parts of his design, but he cannot originate a whole new architectural alphabet. The chances are that he will not find it easy to invent one wholly new moulding. (*Decoration*, 15)

When I read the last quote to Laura Kurgan, an architect, she said, "You could get rid of the molding entirely." It's what the modernists did.

I have discovered the following truth and present it to the world: *cultural evolution is equivalent to the removal of ornament from articles in daily use*. . . . Don't you see the greatness of our age lies in its inability to produce a new form of decoration? We have conquered ornament, we have won through the lack of ornamentation. . . . for ornament is not only produced by criminals; it itself commits a crime, by damaging men's health, the national economy and cultural development.[7]

Adolf Loos wrote his famous essay, or manifesto, "Ornament and Crime," in 1908. Wharton's work on houses and decoration preceded it by a decade. She was in line with Loos, and the modernists, to a point.

It is the superfluous gimcrack – the "ornament" – which is most objectionable, and the more expensive these items are the more likely they are to harm. (*Decoration*, 177)

The supreme excellence is simplicity. Moderation, fitness, relevance . . . There is a sense in which works of art may be said to endure by virtue of that which is left out of them, and it is this "tact of omission" that characterizes the modern-hand. (*Decoration*, 192)

Wharton appreciated simplicity and omission. But she could see the reason, rhythm, and logic of certain kinds of decoration.

While plain panelling, if well-designed, is never out of keeping, the walls of a music-room are specially suited to a somewhat fanciful style of decoration. . . . Fewer changes are possible in the "upright" [piano]; but a marked improvement could be produced by straightening its legs and substituting right angles for the weak curves of the lid. The case itself might be made of plainly panelled mahogany, with a few good ormolu ornaments; or of inlaid wood, with a design of musical instruments . . . (*Decoration*, 146–7)

Slavoj Zizek, lecturing at New York University, once urged the audience I was in to throw out the baby but keep the bathwater. Wharton wanted to keep the bathwater. Her disinclination to throw out everything – except what she called the "horrors" – makes her a vital candidate for rereading and rethinking. Wharton relentlessly forced her characters to live, and die, struggling against or submitting to conventions, acknowledging their contradictions, while trying to create paths through or around rigid social customs. They were usually blocked. She did not imagine a utopia. She didn't see a way of divorcing the past from the present. She didn't see the necessity of abandoning all traditions or styles. Even molding, in proportion to the room, could be beautiful.

It is a curious perversion of artistic laws that has led certain critics to denounce painted architecture or woven mouldings. As in imaginative literature the author may present to his reader as possible anything that he has the talent to make the reader accept, so in decorative art the artist is justified in presenting to the eye whatever his skill can devise to satisfy its requirements; nor is there any insincerity in this proceeding. (*Decoration*, 40)

Her ideas were modern – she wanted to clear the house of nineteenth-century vestiges, stuffed chairs and stuffed shirts, to question conventions and numbing, absurd traditions, but she was far from being a card-carrying modernist. Wharton was skeptical about the new, not positive that progress was progress, not sanguine about the future or the joys of speed and flight, as the futurists were. She took off and looked back over her shoulder at the past. She believed that "original vision is never much afraid of using accepted forms." Maybe she was presciently postmodern. She doesn't fit comfortably into the modernist canon and has suffered for it.

Architecture articulates space, the movement within walls and without them, delineates the relationships of the built to the unbuilt and surroundings. Wharton's prose makes its own particular space, its complex borders pierced by new and old. It's one of those uncanny pieces of fate – less colloquially, historical overdetermination – that her reputation, her literary place, is inflected not just by her idiosyncratic relationship to Modernism but also by three biographical facts: she was female, upper-class, and Henry James's younger friend. Not mentioning James in relation to her is like not mentioning the elephant in the room, a room which she did not, of course, design. Her critical reputation stands mostly in his large shadow. (Her primary biographer R. W. B. Lewis's first sentence in his introduction to *The House of Mirth* begins "Henry James . . .").[8] Few U.S. writers, who are women, make it, as the song goes, to standing in the shadows of love, critical love. (And her books were about love, its promise and seductiveness, its inevitable impossibility within a harsh, prohibitive world.)

The ironist Wharton might have appreciated, in her perverse way, the secondary or minor position she has attained. (Perhaps in the way Deleuze and Guattari appreciate minor literature.) Ironically, undidactically, Wharton teaches that separate isn't equal; difference shouldn't be but usually is hierarchical, and change in any establishment or tradition is, like her sentences, slow.

ACKNOWLEDGMENTS

The author would like to thank Gregg Bordowitz and Kenneth Frampton for their invaluable help in the writing of this essay.

A brief, preliminary version of this essay appeared in *Conjunctions: 29, Tributes, Fall 1997* (pp. 122–125); it was entitled "Edith Wharton: A Mole in the House of the Modern."

NOTES

1. Edith Wharton and Ogden Codman, Jr., *The Decoration of Houses* (New York: Classical America and Henry Hope Reed/Norton, 1998); first published in 1897.
2. Edith Wharton, *The Writing of Fiction* (New York: Touchstone, 1997); first published in 1924.
3. Sigmund Freud, "Contributions to the Psychology of Love," in *Sexuality and the Psychology of Love*, ed. Phillip Rieff (New York: Collier Books, 1963), 63.

4. Edith Wharton, *The Letters of Edith Wharton,* ed. R. W. B. Lewis and Nancy Lewis (New York: Scribner's, 1988), 450–1.

5. Sigmund Freud, "On Narcissism: An Introduction," in *A General Selection from the Words of Sigmund Freud,* ed. John Rickman, M. D. (New York: Doubleday, 1957), 116.

6. Charles Baudelaire, *Intimate Journals,* trans. Christopher Isherwood (London: Picador, 1990), 14.

7. Adolf Loos, "Ornament and Crime," in *Adolf Loos: Pioneer of Modern Architecture,* ed. Ludwig Münz and Gustav Kunstler (New York: Prager, 1966), 226–8.

8. R. W. B. Lewis, "Introduction" to Edith Wharton, *The House of Mirth* (New York: Bantam, 1984), viii.

Notes on Contributors

Deborah Esch, Associate Professor of English at the University of Toronto, is the author of *In the Event: Reading Journalism, Reading Theory* (1999) and *The Brevity of Life* (forthcoming). She is co-editor of *The Turn of the Screw* (Norton Critical Edition, 1999) and *Critical Encounters* (1994), and has published a range of articles on nineteenth- and twentieth-century American and comparative literature, literary theory, media culture, and visual art.

Thomas Loebel is an Assistant Professor of English at the University of Calgary. His research explores the function of literary language at the intersection of philosophy and psychoanalysis, with interests particularly in the constructions of justice and gender. He has recently published on morphology and masculinity in William Faulkner's *Absalom, Absalom!* and is currently completing a book on identity and the subject in American literary modernism.

Mary Nyquist teaches English, Women's and Gender Studies, and Comparative Literary Studies at the University of Toronto, Coeditor, with Margaret Ferguson, of *Re-Membering Milton*, she is the author of numerous essays on early modern literature and on contemporary popular culture and poetry. She is currently completing a study of early modern republicanism and colonialism.

Lynne Tillman's novels include *Haunted Houses, Cast in Doubt, Motion Sickness,* and, most recently, *No Lease on Life,* a National Book Critics Circle Finalist in 1998. She is the author of two fiction collections, *The Madame Realism Complex* and *Absence Makes the Heart*. Her nonfiction includes *The Broad Picture*, an essay collection, and *The Velvet Years: Warhol's Factory 1965–1967*.

Ruth Bernard Yeazell is Chace Family Professor of English at Yale University. Her most recent books are *Fictions of Modesty: Women and Courtship in the English Novel* and *Harems of the Mind: Passages of Western Art and Literature*.

Selected Bibliography

The essays in this collection refer to the 1905 edition of *The House of Mirth*, published by Charles Scribner's Sons. They cite the pagination provided by the Norton Critical Edition of 1990, edited by Elizabeth Ammons, which reprints the 1905 text.

The notes following each chapter yield further references to critical writings on the novel.

Ammons, Elizabeth. *Edith Wharton's Argument with America*. Athens, Ga.: University of Georgia Press, 1990.

Ammons, Elizabeth (ed.). *The House of Mirth*. New York: W.W. Norton, 1990.

Benstock, Shari (ed.). *The House of Mirth*. Boston: Bedford Books, 1994.

Bloom, Harold (ed.). *Modern Critical Views: Edith Wharton*. New York: Chelsea House, 1986.

Davidson, Cathy N. "Kept Women in *The House of Mirth*." *Markham Review* 9 (1979), 10–13.

Dimock, Wai-chee. "Debasing Exchange: Edith Wharton's *The House of Mirth*." *PMLA* 100 (October 1985), 783–92.

Fetterley, Judith. "The Temptation to Be a Beautiful Object: Double Standard and Double Bind in *The House of Mirth*." *Studies in American Fiction* 5 (1977), 199–211.

Gargano, James W. "*The House of Mirth*: Social Futility and Faith." *American Literature* 44 (1972), 137–43.

Gubar, Susan. "'The Blank Page' and the Issues of Female Creativity," in *Writing and Sexual Difference*, ed. Elizabeth Abel. Chicago: University of Chicago Press, 1982.

Howe, Irving (ed.). *Edith Wharton: A Collection of Critical Essays*. Englewood Cliffs, N.J.: Prentice-Hall, 1962.

Kaplan, Amy. "Crowded Spaces in *The House of Mirth*," in her *The Social*

Construction of American Realism. Chicago: University of Chicago Press, 1988.

Lewis, R. W. B. *Edith Wharton: A Biography.* New York: Harper and Row, 1975.

Norris, Margot. "Death by Speculation: Deconstructing *The House of Mirth*," in Benstock, 431–46.

Ozick, Cynthia. "Justice (Again) to Edith Wharton." *Commentary* (October 1976), 48–57.

Poirier, Richard. "Edith Wharton's *The House of Mirth*," in his *The American Novel: From James Fenimore Cooper to William Faulkner.* New York: Basic Books, 1965. Expanded rpt. in his *A World Elsewhere: The Place of Style in American Literature.* New York: Oxford University Press, 1966.

Restuccia, Frances L. "The Name of the Lily: Edith Wharton's Feminism(s)." *Contemporary Literature* 28:2 (Summer 1987), 222–38. Rpt. in Benstock, 404–18.

Rooke, Constance. "Beauty in Distress: *Daniel Deronda* and *The House of Mirth*." *Women and Literature* 4:2 (1976), 28–39.

Showalter, Elaine. "The Death of the Lady (Novelist): Wharton's *House of Mirth*." *Representations* 9 (Winter 1989), 133–49.

Steiner, Wendy. "The Cause of Effect: Edith Wharton and the Economics of Ekphrasis." *Poetics Today* 10 (Summer 1989), 279–97.

Tintner, Adeline R. "Two Novels of 'The Relatively Poor': *New Grub Street* and *The House of Mirth*." *Notes on Modern American Literature* 6:2 (Autumn 1982): item 12.

Trilling, Diana. "*The House of Mirth* Revisited." *Harper's Bazaar* 81 (December 1947), 126–7, 181–6. Rpt. in Howe, 103–18.

Wilson, Edmund. "Justice to Edith Wharton," in *The Wound and the Bow.* New York: Oxford University Press, 1947. Rpt. in Howe, 19–31.

Wolff, Cynthia Griffin. *A Feast of Words: The Triumph of Edith Wharton.* New York: Oxford University Press, 1977.